MARKETING
ME

A Complete Plan to Keep Your Job in Any Economy

By
Douglas J. Wolf

Marketing Me

First printing 2009

Written and Designed by Douglas J. Wolf
Cover Design by:

Kevershan Design
Testerman Communications

Disclaimer

This book is designed to provide information in regard to the subject matter covered. It is sold with the understanding that the publisher and author are not engaged in rendering legal, accounting or other professional services. It is not the purpose of this book to reprint all the information that is otherwise available to the reader but to complement, amplify and supplement other texts. Every effort has been make to make this book as accurate as possible. However, there may be mistakes both typographical and in content. Therefore, this text should be used only as a general guide and not as the ultimate source of self-improvement information. Furthermore, this book contains up to date information as of the printing date. The purpose of this manual is to educate and entertain. The author and publisher shall have neither liability nor responsibility to any person or entity with respect to loss or damage caused or alleged to be caused, directly or indirectly by the information contained in this book.

If you do not wish to be bound by the above, you may return this book to the publisher.

Dedication

I hereby dedicate this book to my eternal grandmother Pearl Wolf. She is a daily inspiration.

Acknowledgments

Gloria Wolf – my behind the scenes creative mind
Abe Arkeen –editor extraordinaire

Who Should Read this Book

If you are:

- Currently employed but not directly responsible for generating revenue
- Categorized as overhead or "general/administrative,"
- Under the impression that just doing your job well will shelter you from lay-offs.

You may be deemed expendable and you need to put an action plan together now! This book provides the vital actions and professional guidance required for you to take control and preserve your job.

Most people labor under the illusion that if they do their job well, that is enough. They are dead wrong. We are living in extraordinary economic times and what worked in the past is not enough today. I explore this further in Chapter One.

Consider your workplace. Are there coworkers who have been promoted over you when they did not work nearly as hard or are not competent in their job areas? Do you ever wonder why that happens?

In this book, I examine why those individuals are getting ahead of you and retaining their jobs over you. It is unlikely that they are particularly brilliant or have invented a new way of doing business. What they have done is figured out the real goal of their job and how to best achieve it.

These coworkers have figured out how to constantly market their skills to the boss. You can to as a result of reading this book.

Who Should Not Read this Book

- If you are the owner/CEO/President of a business and have employees, buy this book and give it to *them*. It will help your business survive and prosper because they will become better at what they do for you.

- If you are in sales, your value is easier to quantify. So you might not need this book. But you might find it useful to further your career.

One More Point

While keeping your job is your most important goal, know that making your boss look good is also vital. These are mutually reinforcing goals. The more you do the things I recommend, the better your boss will be perceived by *his* boss, helping him keep his job, which in turn will help you keep your job.

Foreword

To Managers and Supervisors: How to keep valuable employees

Most employees do not want to lose their jobs or be forced to change employers. I encourage you to use the concepts in this book to work *with* your current team members to improve, where needed, their abilities to produce good work and promote their value. Doing so will make your job easier and less likely that you will lose *your* job.

For instance, managers who want to retain employees should look at what behaviors they reward and how respectfully they treat their team members. These are the basic premises of most leadership treatises and have held true through years of research, including hundreds of polls as well as anecdotal evidence of great leaders and happy employees. Reward the behaviors that are valuable to the company and treat everyone with the respect you expect and you will keep good employees.

However, most managers do not follow this advice and find they are surrounded by *slightly* resourceful, *somewhat* creative, *semi-* loyal, *mostly* productive employees: In other words, a team of average performers. You – and they – deserve and can do more.

My advice is simple: give them this book. It will help them understand that by making your job easier and less complicated, they help you look good to your boss, which in turn, helps them retain their jobs. And you retain your job.

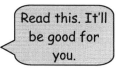

Read this. It'll be good for you.

While what I recommend may at first appear superficial or "for show" only, the truth of the workplace is that perception is reality. Everyone has the ability to manage how they are perceived by others and therefore increase their value. If you really think about it and peel back the layers, you *know* this and you have engaged in these activities yourself – because they work! They are not hollow or false: they are truthful presentations of your contributions and those of your team.

©2009 by Douglas J. Wolf

Better that YOU manage the material that gets in front of bosses and colleagues than that you let others do your speaking for you. If you truly believe that the work you do is worthwhile, then it is also worth your time and effort to help others recognize that quality as well.

Use this book and the subsequent efforts by your employees to improve your standing, increase their allegiance to you, retain a good team of employees and make your company a better place to work. By implementing the ideas I recommend, you will all work together more effectively. Consequently, you will produce better results that others know about and admire which is the *best* way to keep your job.

> *The man who doesn't read good books has no advantage over the man who can't read them.*
> *Mark Twain (1835 - 1910)*

To Male and Female Readers

There are different viewpoints, based on gender, in some of the recommendations and ideas in this book. Some of them are due to the different ways men's and women's brains process and then communicate information. I believe there *are* basic differences in men's and women's brains. I also recognize that these differences fall on a continuum rather than belonging to one or the other gender. I encourage you, the reader, to include that consideration in your use of the Marketing Me techniques and tactics so that you incorporate words and phrases appropriate into your communication to more effectively reach the man or women to whom you are speaking.

 To help you do this I have included bothviewpoints. Sometimes you will be able to pick them out easily because they are overtly laid out; men and women approach situations differently and use different words to communicate. (See Chapter 2, for instance, in the section titled, "Mistakes Women Make.") Other times, I include the different perspectives more subtlety, such as when I offer a variety of sample conversations about one topic. Some use words that men are more likely to use, other times, the word choices are more likely to be what a woman would say.

I interchange the use of him/her throughout the book to refer to your Boss. This randomness is purposeful and intended to be inclusive. It is not intended to indicate that the examples of how to speak to your boss in that chapter or section are directed at one gender. You should ascertain which communication style your boss prefers (see Chapter 3) and then incorporate the differences in gender as they fit.

I am more than happy to provide coaching resources for you on this powerful yet challenging skill set. Refer to the Epilogue for more information and how to contact me.

Respectfully,

The Author:
Douglas J. Wolf

Marketing Me

Table of Contents

Chapter One: Marketing Me in Seven Steps

In this chapter, I introduce you to the Seven Steps of your Marketing Me plan of action. I also make the case, based on facts, that you must take action now to save your job.

A Hard Look at the Facts

An economic crisis shook the world in the fall of 2008. The subsequent layoffs and work force reductions should focus the mind of everyone who has a job on an essential task - **keeping that job**.

A False Sense of Security

Many of you reading this may be living in the land of denial, thinking that the job you do is so crucial that your company could not survive without you. Nonsense! What would happen if you suffered a severe health problem and could not work? Do you really believe your company would fail if you were not there?

In 1933, during the Great Depression, over 25% of the US population was out of work. Right now, no one is predicting that a depression is inevitable, but the possibility has to be considered. It is likely that unemployment will reach levels higher than they have been in a very long time.

It's going to take a lo-ong time...

The economy is not going to recover quickly from this mess. Despite what happens in Washington D.C., business cycles cannot be significantly shortened or eliminated. Politicians will speak in serious tones and spend your money in outrageous ways, but government cannot reverse this problem. Only time can, and it will get worse before it gets better. You need to take action sooner rather than later before things do get worse.

You have work ahead of you in order to keep your job.

Decision Time

You have to decide if you are going to do your utmost to keep the job you have or become a victim of the current job implosion. Even if unemployment were to hit 25%, 75% of the population would still be at work.

In this book, you get the tools to be in that 75%.

Whatever you decide, at the very least implementing even a portion of my advice will result in a better working relationship with your boss.

Marketing Me: the Seven Steps

The Seven Steps of Marketing Me were gleaned from the writings of several marketing gurus and articles by dozens of career advice authors as well as my own experience.

A summary of Marketing Me the Seven Steps is below.

Step 1: Change your Mindset

The Marketing Me mindset is proactive, responsible and innovative. Step 1: Change your Mindset, states *you* must make known to your company your value and contributions. In Chapter 2 and Chapter 3 I challenge you to think about how you present your value to your boss. I provide examples and activities to move you from complacency to action, from timidity to boldness.

Step 2: Understand your Marketing Me Target Market: Your Boss

Step 2 is in covered in Chapter 4. This chapter delivers proven tools for understanding how your boss likes to receive and give information. You learn how to talk with your boss so that you seem more *like* your boss. You become adept at communicating with her; therefore she wants to keep you around.

Mini-me?!

Step 3: Build Your Own Performance Review

Chapter 5 provides a plan of action to collect achievements, testimonials and measurable results into your own performance review portfolio. Step 3 is crucial to your job-keeping success. I recommend building your own review so that when your performance comes under scrutiny – such as during a lay off – you have tangible evidence of your irreplaceable value to the organization.

Step 4: Campaign for Yourself: Your Micro Marketing Me activities

Chapter 6 focuses on Step 4 of your Marketing Me campaign. I show you how to craft a personal marketing message that highlights your skills, knowledge and contributions to your company. I emphasize the key concept to understanding why you must implement these activities: Managing your Boss' perception of your value.

Step 5: Campaign for Yourself: Big Marketing Me activities

Job keepers are expert at blowing their own horn at work, the subject of Step 5. In Chapter 7, I show you even more ways to raise your internal profile in a positive way. You will get ideas on how to make many others, not just your boss, aware of your expertise. This makes him look good for keeping you on his team.

Step 6: Align Your Skills with the Needs of your Company

You may be the best employee your company ever had. But the minute your skills or knowledge become slightly out of date, your job is at risk. In Chapter 8, I explain how to align the presentation of your skills with the needs of your company as it goes through predictable business cycles. Marketing Me is proactive, so Step 6 in your Marketing Me plan puts you ahead of your coworkers and on top of business trends that could affect your job.

Step 7: Organize your Marketing Me Campaign

My Marketing Me plan for you is comprehensive. Chapter 9 provides directions and tools to help you organize and plan your Marketing Me activities. Step 7 is your call to action: Put your Marketing Me activities in your schedule and incorporate them into everyday. Only with this kind of persistence and consistency will you succeed at keeping your job in this economy. Chapter 10 addresses the common excuses and reasons people do not change their way of presenting their attributes. Reading this chapter will inspire you to be one of the successful Marketing Me implementers. You become a job keeper.

> *Time and tide wait for no man.*
>
> *Geoffrey Chaucer*

It may seem daunting at this point to put all seven steps into practice. There are tools throughout the book to keep you focused. In the Resources section on my website I offer additional tools. Keeping your job does take significant effort and dedicated time and planning. If you want to keep your job, choose to invest in yourself.

Where You Stand Today: Take Inventory

Take a Close Look At Your Company

- If your company is in a business that supplies a product or service that is *optional* for many people, be wary. For example, the residential real estate industry is likely to be depressed for several more years. Any business that relies on home sales is going to suffer. Another example is the luxury goods market where demand has fallen off sharply.

Take a very close look...

Examine Your Market

- What is your firm's position in its industry?

- Is your particular company a leader or an also-ran?

- Does the company leadership understand the challenges presented by this severe downturn? Are they responding intelligently to preserve the firm?

- Is the water cooler chatter positive or negative? Is your company already laying off workers?

- Check the company website and any publications. Ask the salespeople their opinion of the health of the business. They likely have the most up to date information based on customer relations and daily revenue results.

Assess Your Role

- Take a hard look at your role in the firm. If your company provides basic goods or services and you are not directly involved in generating sales, your job could be disposable. This is a hard fact to believe for many people. They seem to think that if they do their job as they always have they will be protected from the layoff axe. This is very far from the truth. Many case studies from past recessions demonstrate that adequately doing your job is just not enough.

Lost Job Costs

For every $10,000 in salary you earned at your former job, assume one month of new job search time and lost income. Five months of job searching for an employee who formerly earned $50,000 is nearly $21,000 lost! It is much cheaper to stay in your current job than to have to research which companies are hiring, discover what kind of skills and employees they seek, and then parade through a series of agonizing interviews. Instead of wasting time and money in a new job search, invest in keeping your job.

> *The VP of Training for a training company that was significantly in debt and had no new business on the horizon thought she did not need to promote her value to her boss. After all she worked for a training company and she was the highest level trainer! Even knowing the financials and the lack of cash flow, she believed her job was secure. She diligently worked on projects at hand, pitched in on projects others had let fall because they were doing "other" work, and stayed out of the way of the CEO who was frantically trying to get new business. Much to her surprise, she got laid off. When she asked why she was let go while the people who did the "other" work were not, she was told their work was more valuable to the company. Obviously, what she had contributed was not known or valued. After licking her wounds, she realized how she had neglected to heed the warnings and advice of others who told her to do everything she could to make her boss appreciate and value her contributions.*

Take Action Now!

If it is obvious from your review of your company that it is headed for difficult times, or that the job you have is one that could go away if cutbacks occur, start implementing my recommendations *now*. Many people are emotionally paralyzed and wait too long before starting to protect their jobs. **TOO LATE.**

Marketing Your Self to your Company

I am introducing you to an idea that is a radical departure from how you probably think about your working career. I believe that in order to stay employed and, more importantly, to better your position, you have to think of yourself as a service provider to your company and, most significantly, to your boss. While you may be the nicest person around the office, the fact is that what you are *paid* must be less than what you *produce* <u>and</u> your boss has to believe it. You have to prove you are a good return on your company's investment in you.

You may believe that you are paid far less than the profit you contribute to the company. But, the smart employees - the job keepers - make certain that the most important person in the company, their boss, knows this too.

> *When we are no longer able to change a situation...we are challenged to change ourselves.*
>
> *Victor Frankl*

Know, Like and Trust

You want your boss to know, like and trust you. I am not suggesting that you are going to try to become best friends with your boss. I am suggesting that Marketing Me gives you the tools to create a stronger, highly collaborative relationship with your boss.

> **Know:** Your boss understands and values your contribution to the firm.

> **Like:** Your boss feels that he can effectively communicate with you. He feels comfortable working with you in any situation and you behave appropriately at all times. You are, in the context of business, *like* him, and this can develop a lasting, profitable relationship.

> **Trust:** Your boss believes you when you say that you have taken care of a problem. He does not have to always check up on your work. He knows that you anticipate problems and handle them without always consulting him. On the other hand, he knows that if a problem arises that needs his input that you will bring it to his attention. He knows that in chatting with co-workers you support his ideas and decisions and carry them out.

I assume you are competent at your job because if that were not true all the techniques in the world will probably not get your boss to trust you and keep you on his payroll.

Faking It?

It is important to note that Marketing Me techniques are not manipulative actions, or a collection of good deeds that build up so you can call them in when you need a favor. In Stephen Covey's book, <u>The Seven Habits of Highly Effective People</u>, he describes a concept called the **emotional bank account** and the types of behaviors that build a reserve of mutual trust. These are sincere, freely given gestures of appreciation, support, and interest in the well-being of the other person, in this case, your boss. (By extension, your actions demonstrate dedication to your company's well-being.)

My assertion is that your goal is to make your boss look good. Pursued with clarity and genuineness, the actions I am suggesting you take throughout this book will build a solid relationship in which your boss knows, likes, trusts and KEEPS you.

> *Treat every person with kindness and respect, even those who are rude to you. Remember that you show compassion to others not because of who they are but because of who you are.*
>
> *Andrew T. Somers*

Are you ready?

If you agree with us and all the experts who predict the U.S. economy is in for a rough ride for several years, then you must take action and put my recommended job-keeping ideas into practice. On the other hand, if you think this is a short term situation and keeping your head down and your nose to the grind stone will keep you employed, you do not need to read this book. There are plenty of books out there that will tell you how to *find* your next job.

Summary

In this chapter I made it clear that you must take action today to keep your job. I presented the Seven Steps of your Marketing Me plan that will enable you to very quickly change the way your boss perceives you as an employee. Implementing these steps will enhance how he is perceived by others due to your efforts to make him look good. You become a job keeper.

Next Chapter

In the following chapters, I reveal actions for each of the Seven Steps. I describe the tools and recommend techniques to implement on a daily basis to enhance your chances of staying employed.

It is best that you read this book in the order presented. Skipping ahead is not going be useful unless you clearly understand the previous Step and what you should do with that information.

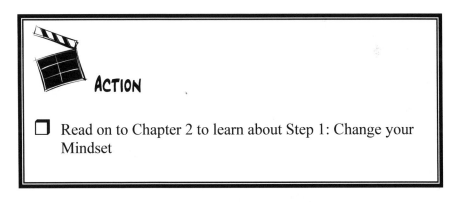

ACTION

☐ Read on to Chapter 2 to learn about Step 1: Change your Mindset

> *It is not necessary to change. Survival is not mandatory.*
> *W. Edwards Deming*

How We Got Here: An optional read

The media typically does its best to exaggerate any problem into a crisis, but this economic collapse is a real crisis. If you are unclear about what really happened, read on.

In the past five years or so, millions of Americans were lent money for home purchases even when they really could not afford the monthly payments. Those mortgages were then bundled and sold to investors around the world. The buyers of the bundled mortgages expected income every month from all the individual mortgage payments.

But then three things happened. First, housing prices started falling as part of the natural cycle of real estate. Secondly, gas prices rose quickly in the spring of 2008. Suddenly, millions of homeowners could not pay their house payments and pay for expensive gas for their cars and heating. Thirdly, many of the owners had adjustable rate mortgages and the monthly payments went up very steeply. Faced with either buying food and gas or making the house payment on a property *losing* value, homeowners choose to stop paying the mortgage.

Suddenly with no or reduced payments coming in, the owners of the bonds could not pay *their* bills and so on. And their vendors, who were expecting regular payments, were suddenly short of cash. The banks that used to readily extend them short-term credit to pay bills stopped giving those loans. The whole engine screeched to a halt.

While that was bad, a large insurance company, AIG, had sold insurance contracts guaranteeing that if the mortgage holders did not make their payments, AIG would cover those payments. However, AIG never reserved any money to pay any of those potential claims. When claims were filed to collect on their insurance, the mortgage bond holders were told, "Sorry we lied to you; we do not have any money to pay you."

> Sorry!
> No money!

Within days, no one was sure if they were going to get payments on any of the bonds they held, and, as it turned out, a large portion were not. Bond companies laid off thousands of workers. Across both the American and world economy, the crisis spread. People in every line of work started to worry about job security and stopped spending.

With over 2 million jobs lost in 2008 and layoffs continuing in 2009, the prognosis for the short term future is more of the same. Some economists are predicting a 10% or more unemployment rate before recovery takes hold. A recovery of any strength could take several years as all that mortgage debt is paid off.

Chapter Two
Step 1: Part 1 Change How You Think About Your Job

In this chapter, I tell you how to correctly think about your job in order to keep it. This is the first part of Step 1

Most employees believe their work is valued. They also believe that *they* are valued. You probably make this same error in logic, an error that can breed complacency. If you assume your boss values you and your work, you will not promote yourself and your achievements.

The underlying false belief is that you will keep your job because you are valued for the *work* you do. In fact, the work you do can be done by someone else *with very few exceptions*.

Here is the hard truth: If you were out of commission (injured or ill) for six months, your work would get done by others. Perhaps not in the same way as you would do it or as well done as you, but it would get done. Ultimately, your employer cares about that one thing: The <u>work</u> gets done and revenue is not significantly interrupted or affected.

This is the reason *you* are at risk of losing your job.

The NY Times reported on January 26th, 2009 that Home Depot, Caterpillar, Sprint, Nextel and at least eight other well-established companies, companies that were thriving in 2008, would cut more than 75,000 jobs in the United States and around the world.

Your Proactive Mindset

The Marketing Me mindset is proactive. Make no assumptions about the value of you or your work. Your ongoing primary priority is to make sure the decision makers in your company are aware of and pleased with your work: In other words, they know you are a "keeper."

To accomplish that, you need to do your work and do it well. If your performance is an issue, get help now to improve it. Implementing my Marketing Me concepts and activities can improve your chances of keeping your job. But, do not assume my recommendations will insure your job if you are an obvious sub-performer.

> *Tip:* make no assumptions about how much others value you or your work

There are situations, we all know, where people who are completely incompetent keep their jobs. You may know employees who are also family members, who got in on the ground floor or are sacred cows: They are untouchable. But others workers who are keeping their jobs are probably doing the activities I am about to recommend to you. That is why *they* are job keepers!

Managing others' perceptions

Marketing Me is a mindset of proactively promoting you and your work to the right people at the right time in the right way. Make managing other's perceptions of you, including your boss', your top priority.

> Number 1 Job: Look Good.

Once you have the mindset of promoting yourself, you will create new ideas and notice opportunities to speak up or interject a comment about the value of your work. Our minds are wonderful search engines. For example, have you noticed when you buy a car that you suddenly notice how many other people are driving the same car? Or, try this: Pick a word for the day, such as horse or flag. You will notice *that* word more than you would have if you had not chosen the word. Your "search engine" brain works automatically to find it. Your Marketing Me mindset works like that. Once you tune your mind to seeking and taking advantage of situations where you can promote yourself and your work, you will find them.

The most likely situations when you can begin your quest to influence other's perceptions are meetings, formal or informal. Project update meetings are excellent opportunities because you can speak up and help others become more aware of how the work you are doing is moving the project forward and achieve objectives. Even if your boss, your target market, does not attend, it is necessary to impress upon the people in the meetings who may report back to him how you have made valuable contributions to the project.

> *Know your boss's pains, and make their life easy. If you make your boss's lives easy, they will embrace you and keep you near.*
> Brent Neilsen, Leadership Development Consultant,
> quoted on LinkedIn

Re-Frame Your Input

You are probably already contributing great ideas and advice for projects and adding your input to decision-making discussions. The key change you are about to make is in how you re-frame your input. No longer will you offer ideas without first framing up these three concepts:

1. Why **you** are the expert on your idea or contribution,
2. That you **know** it is a great idea or that it contributes to the success of the project, and
3. You understand the **strategic** importance of the item under discussion.

This example illustrates reframing your message: (The numbers refer to the three points above.)

> **You:** "Jeff, I'm sure we need the exact component specified here because *1)* I was in on this from the beginning, and *2)* I tested each component. I knew this was an *3)* important part of the entire project, so I was very thorough, not wanting to hold it up down the road. My recommendation is..."

The key is to be assertive with your knowledge and expertise without being argumentative or condescending.

Some cautions:

- Never speak about your achievements as a means to put down others. Doing so is perceived as insecure or undignified.
- Do not criticize the work of others while asserting the value of your work: comparisons are unnecessary when you have managed how others perceive the value of your work. By being proactive and promoting yourself and your work, you rise above comparison.
- Openly establish that you support the project and/or the project leader (or discussion leader), even if disagreements arise during project discussions.

When you report your contributions to a project, be sure to tie your achievements back to the major objectives of the project. Re-frame your input.

> *If the marketplace isn't talking about you, there's a reason. If people aren't discussing your products, your services, your cause, your movement or your career, there's a reason. The reason is that you're boring.*
>
> *Seth Godin, author*
> *Blogpost*

Here are two more examples:

You: Since our last update, I've completed items 3 and 4 **on time** and **within budget**, which helped Team G finish their part. This helps us make sure we **deliver this to the customer** on time – maybe even ahead of time.

OR

You: In that part of the project, I referred to my experience on the Gold project to come up with a way to solve the supply chain problem, specifically mapping out the exact location of every part needed to

I made a difference.

make repairs to the Vital Machine, and setting up an inventory tracking system within 3 days. Problem solved. **The customer is very happy**.

During discussions of new projects, there are ample opportunities to impart your relevant knowledge and experience. Listen for an opening and confidently speak up with how you successfully did that kind of work in the past or participated in a similar initiative.

Like this:

You: I remember building a **similar solution** for Keene Company and they were **ecstatic**. I'll look at that project file for the specifics so we can move ahead quickly. Let's meet in two days to discuss that.

OR

You: Your idea, Greg, has some merit, because when I worked on the proposal for Halverson, I included a **similar provision** and it **flew through**. We should look at that proposal and use it as a basis for this one. Will two o'clock today work for you?

Take advantage of re-framing your input whenever these situations arise. Interject information that specifically delineates *what* you know, *why* you know it and *how* it helps the project.

Fine Tune Your Words

Another way to promote yourself is to offer up short stories in informal situations. These brief messages are easy to use and powerful.

> Remember every job is a self-portrait of the person who did it.
> Autograph your work with excellence.
> James A. Brewer

Now that your mind is finding the opportunities to say them, be ready with a handful of fine-tuned anecdotes about how you have contributed to the organization or project. Anecdotes – short stories - create interest and curiosity.

Before you speak up though, rehearse your phrases or stories so they easily and concisely flow into a conversation. Follow these simple fine-tuning guidelines:

1. Carefully choose your words
2. Practice altering your tone of voice so you do not sound like you are groveling, arrogant, or even worse, uncertain
3. Alter the pace of your speaking so that you do not sound hesitant or stilted
4. Rehearse. Practice the stories and phrases out loud, repeat them, change and rearrange words until saying them is comfortable for you.
5. Strive to sound natural.

Practice while driving, in front of a mirror, while exercising, and so on. Try your anecdotes on friends, your partner, even your kids. Look for a question or a request to say more which means you have generated enough interest that someone wants to learn more.

You may be acquainted with the concept of creating an "elevator speech." Elevator speeches are intended to promote you to strangers. Marketing Me messages, on the other hand, are to promote your *work* to people who do know you but may not know the value of your work…yet. Both are brief and naturally said, hence the necessity for fine tuning your words. Be confident that you believe what you are saying. I tell you more on how to do this in <u>Chapter 6</u>.

To venture causes anxiety, but not to venture is to lose oneself.
Senator Orrin G. Hatch

"But I feel weird bragging about myself…"

Get over it! The job keepers in your company do it without a second thought because they know they *must* promote themselves to keep their jobs and get promoted. This notion that talking about yourself is boastful will hinder your progress and could put your job in jeopardy.

An important skill you must put into play everyday is the ability to provide the decision makers with data and impressions that make them decide to keep you. Bosses who have to make lay-off decisions under stress and imminent deadlines need to know they are making the right decisions: Their jobs depend on it. Helping them do this is your job.

No one else is going to "brag" for you and no one else will brag about you with more finesse and fervor than you. It is a myth that others take notice of us: Fame is fleeting. Others think about *themselves* – as you do – more than 99% of the time, leaving little room to consider what you are up to or how they can help you. Brag about yourself. You can not count on someone else to do your advertising for you. Develop the mindset that this project belongs only to you. Get over feeling weird, reluctant or hesitant about self-promotion. Make it a habit to seek opportunities to promote your achievements and skills, especially to the person whose opinion of you matters most: your boss.

> We probably wouldn't worry about what people think of us if we could know how seldom they do.
> Olin Miller

Mistakes Women Make

The overarching habits women tend to have in the self-promoting arena are "team-think" and the inclination to build relationship webs versus the more male tendencies to direct the team and win the game.

Women impair their images as leaders and achievers by committing these errors:

Making indirect or cushy statements; posing ideas as questions versus statement

- "I think we should…" *versus* "We should…"
- "I'm pretty sure that won't work…" *versus* "That's not advisable and here's why."
- "Don't you think it's better if…" *versus* "This way is more effective because..."
- "Are you sure?" *versus* "That doesn't match my information."

Adding an explanation or demure statements when responding to a compliment or praise, or not taking the opportunity to *tell* them to advocate for you

"Thank you" is a complete sentence.

- "Thanks. It's wasn't that big of a deal." *versus* "Thank you. I worked very hard on this."
- "Thank you, you're too generous." *versus* "Thank you."
- "I appreciate that. Would you be willing to tell Mr. Big Guy?" *versus* "Thank you. Please let Mr. Phillips know what I accomplished here."

Not cashing in your chips

Getting ahead is a quid pro quo (Latin meaning, "something for something") game. In other words, I scratch your back. I expect and will ask you to scratch mine. Women tend to expect others to be generous, as they would, with praise of others' work. However, a competitor does not promote his competition, and, in fact, will more likely seek opportunities to, subtly or blatantly, undermine the success of others if it will help them win. This economy promotes more competition for which you must be ready.

If you help someone, assume you will need to *ask* them to help you look good to your boss. Do not hesitate to do so.

For example:

You stay late to finish your part of a presentation to help a male colleague meet a deadline that was changed. When you agree to help, make sure you say, "I expect payback."

Women impair their images as leaders and achievers by presenting the team as the achiever versus asserting the value of their personal *leadership*.

Several weeks later, you tell this same colleague to support your request to take on additional responsibility, reminding him that he owes you. Note: cash your chips judiciously and wisely. It is poor judgment to use them to ask someone to cover for you while you leave work in the middle of the day for a personal appointment.

Also, at the end of the projects, ask this colleague to send you an email thanking you for the extra effort. Forward (or cc) it to your Boss. This is an example of how you collect testimonials about your work, which I discuss further in Chapter 5.

Not telling people you want a promotion or more responsibility

Not revealing your ambition is a mistake. It is relative to expecting others to notice your good work or achievements for their own merit. Never assume your boss knows what you want, and do not believe in the inherent goodness of others to promote your interests. While bighearted things do happen, in this competitive depressed economy, everyone is trying to keep their job. Be upfront, specific and direct concerning your desires for additional responsibilities. Tell your boss and other decision makers and influencers early and often that you are ready, willing and able.

Believing you need to have everyone like you in order to succeed

This concept is not quite as black and white as "being *liked* versus being employed." However, many women are reluctant to take a stance that might make others look bad, create resentment or induce envy. They choose to stay quiet instead of disagree. They drop an argument when they know they are right.

When I described a situation where I backed down even when I knew my solution was best, my coach said to me, "Would you rather be liked or get the job done right?" If it is an important business issue, including fighting for your job, reduce your tendency to want to be liked.

> *Be more concerned with your character than with your reputation. Your character is what you really are while your reputation is merely what others think you are.*
> *UCLA Coach John Wooden*

Calibrate your fundamental thinking toward getting what you want even if others are pushed out or weakened in the process. Even Gandhi had enemies. It is likely you have several people in your life who like you. In this awful economy, lean on them for friendship while you pursue your goals. Just do not make an enemy of your boss.

Summary

This chapter discussed the importance of changing how you think about your job as you launch your Marketing Me campaign. You move from letting others drive the perception of your work to taking the wheel and steering a new path for your career.

Next Chapter

In Chapter 3, Step 2 continues and I describe the change of mindset you need to adopt. I also share compelling tactics you can implement immediately to help you keep your job.

ACTION

☐ Make a list of all of the people in your organization who may have an impact on the decision to keep you or not

☐ Prioritize that list by the consequence of their opinions of you: Who heeds their opinions?
- o You may find it more useful to build an organization-type chart or mind map (see example on the next page) of the people on your list to better see the connections and how they wield influence

☐ For each of the top 10 or most influential, create a checklist:
- o What message do you want them to get about your accomplishments, skills, and knowledge?
- o Set a specific date or "after I speak with Mr. Lewis…"? to get your message to them.
- o How will you get that message to them? (Develop several options)

☐ Create a list of at least 10 new and different ways to get your message out in general. More ideas are presented in the following chapters.

☐ Be creative and use your knowledge of your organization and your resources.

☐ Rehearse stories of your achievements until you find them easy to say

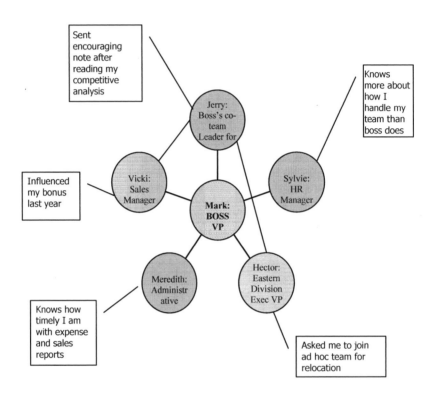

Accept the challenges so that you may feel the exhilaration of victory.
  Gen'l George S. Patton

Chapter Three

Step 1: Part 2 Change Your Mindset

In this chapter, I tell you how important it is to change your mindset in order to put my recommendations into practice and succeed. This is Part 2 of Step 1.

While you are preparing to manage others' perceptions of you, you also want to establish a new mindset. Managing how you think about yourself - your mindset - is a key element of success and a sign of emotional intelligence. Your new mindset is:

Marketing yourself requires you to think of yourself as a product or service that has value to others both in revenue and other tangible results. Most of us would protest that we *do* think of ourselves as valuable. How strong is that perception of you in <u>others'</u> minds? Do they know your value? Do they promote and describe it to others when given the opportunity? Do they think of you and your talents when a particular skill or ability is requested? Until *you* market your value, your value is irrelevant, except perhaps to your Mom.

In the marketing world, there exists a much-maligned phenomenon attributed to ads called, "Marketing for Mom." These ads brag about the features and capabilities of the product or service. "We built it in three days." "No one else comes close." "There's never been anything like it."

Hi Mom!

Such ads tell the audience nothing about how that product will help them: There is no WIIFM (What's In It For Me) for the buyer.

©2009 by Douglas J. Wolf

Most people think of their work accomplishments in the same manner:

- **I** did that.
- **I** was that good.
- **I** fixed that.

Commendable. But how did it help others and how will it help them in the future? That is the Marketing Me mindset you will develop and the message you need to express to your boss and co-workers. When you complete valuable actions, you implement high-level skills and talents and you share expert knowledge that helps others get what they want. If they get what they want, you get what you want, especially your boss. These are the concepts to instill into your everyday thinking.

> You are searching for the magic key that will unlock the door to the source of power; and yet you have the key in your own hands, and you make use of it the moment you learn to control your thoughts.
>
> Napoleon Hill

Mindset management also means you believe in yourself enough to make an effort even when it seems like a long shot, when others are pessimistic about the outcome or when your boss is being a jerk. This is *your* game to win or lose and your mindset is a strong determinant of the outcome.

How to Change your Mindset

To change your Mindset use this powerful tool: Act as if you are what you want to be. Think of yourself as a very important contributor to the results of your organization. Act as if your value is incalculable to your boss and your company.

Dieters learn to think about their relationship with food and change it – from "comforting" to "nutrition." They henceforth use food to feed their bodies, not their feelings. Professional athletes learn to think of their workouts as their job: Olympic Gold Medalist Peter Vidmar says work out when you feel like it, work out when you do not feel like it.

Problem solvers think, "How *can* this work?" versus "Why *won't* this work?" According to recent research about how our minds can develop, even into old age, those simple changes in thinking make an enormous difference in our resourcefulness and creativity.

> *The survival of the fittest is the ageless law of nature, but the fittest are rarely the strong. The fittest are those endowed with the qualifications for adaptation, the ability to accept the inevitable and conform to the unavoidable, to harmonize with existing or changing conditions.*
>
> *Dave E. Smalley, Author*

Changing habits/mindsets is not an overnight transformation. The 24/7/365 work pace and access to information has created an expectation that changes can be instantaneous. Humans have not yet adapted to that idea. We are still creatures of habit.

Just do it, do it, do it...

Assume that you will need to repeat any new behavior at least 30 times before it becomes comfortable, and many more times than that to make it habitual. Keep in mind, the payoff, like a diet, is not instantaneous and you need to persevere. Perseverance is one of the most recognized components of success.

Keep-your-job Activities

The following is a list of keep-your-job activities that get results, starting below and continuing to the end of the chapter. Scan this list. Note those you are already doing, even if you have only done them once or twice. Next, highlight those you want to do, those that seem relevant and applicable to your situation. Also highlight those which may be most attractive to your boss and likely to enhance his standing in the company.

Next, underline or circle two to three that you will implement in the next ten days. Choose only two or three so that you do not overwhelm yourself. They may be the same as those you are already doing and you have chosen to do a better job at them or do them more. Before

you start doing any of these, be sure to assess those you chose. Ask yourself:
- Are they relevant to my boss?
- To the company's objectives?
- Can I do them without drawing unwanted attention to myself?
- Can I do them without taking a lot of time from my priority projects?
- Will they accomplish my objective to present my value to others?

Believe there is no work for the good of the enterprise that is beneath you.

Ruth H. Gilman, Pres of Human Resources Services

On my website, you can download an excel spreadsheet of this list to customize and use for tracking your Marketing Me campaign.

Decrease Conflicts on the Job

When you have a conflict with a co-worker do everything *you* can to resolve it with the other party. If you escalate conflicts to your boss' desk, they may get resolved but you will be branded a trouble-maker who is unable to get along with others and perhaps land on the short list for layoffs.

If you are not confident in your ability to resolve conflicts, get training or coaching. Developing this skill will serve you extremely well professionally and personally.

If you have are fortunate enough to have a boss who is proactive when it comes to conflict, and you have not been able to resolve the issue yourself, you are better served by bringing it to his attention for advice or resolution rather than allowing it to go unresolved. Issues that are swept under the rug always come back to bite. You do not want to surprise him with an old problem that could have been attended to long ago. You want him to see you as a proactive person who solves problems.

Job Example

Deedee was an excellent technical worker who consistently exceeded expectations. However, whenever she worked on a project with men who were on a little higher level than she, disturbing conflicts arose. She and they were not able to resolve them and they caused a lot of discomfort for the other team members because of the constant bickering. After 6 years on the job, she complained to HR that she wasn't getting promoted like others who had been there for less time. The HR Director told her it was because her boss saw her as a difficult person to work with and until that was fixed she would not be considered for promotion. Deedee sought out a coach (Because her boss was obviously not going to help her) to develop her conflict resolution skills. Within a year, no more interpersonal conflicts were escalated because of her and she was promoted.

Use Good Timing

Consider when your boss likes to get information. Even the time of day is a consideration. Does your boss prefer mornings when her energy level is high or later in the day when her desk has cleared? Does she prefer face to face conversations? Is she more comfortable one on one or in groups? Some of the most productive conversations with bosses occur when everyone else has left for the day and there are no possible interruptions.

Perhaps she does not mind the "got a minute?" knock at her office door. If you take advantage of this, be sure what you bring is *truly* important.

Lisa's communication style is informal, chatty, full of story-telling detail and meandering. Some of her colleagues enjoyed this but one of the people above her that she had to work with a lot hated it. He preferred a "just the facts" style. Over time, he sighed and appeared annoyed with her when she appeared at his door to "ask a quick question..." because she wasn't quick. She finally asked him why he acted so impatient with her. He loudly replied, "Just get to the point! I don't have time for all this stuff." Taken aback, Lisa consulted with a colleague who explained that Lisa's style was too chatty and informal for this guy who was an action-oriented, task-focused communicator. Lisa changed her style and brought a list to keep her conversations brief with this manager.

Dress for Job-keeping

Dress like the boss. In flush times, people who wear eyebrow rings and funky clothes might be hired, but when the crunch comes as it is now, unorthodox looks will be seen as non-conformist – something to be tolerated - and likely the first to go. If your boss dresses unconventionally, it is not crucial that you match that; you at least know you could if you wanted to.

Wear clean clothes, keep your nails clean and trimmed, implement good dental hygiene, and keep perfume and cologne to a minimum. The concept is not to conform, it is to <u>not</u> distract. You want people to value your work, not the thrill of your outfit display, unless you are in a business that *does* value unconventional dress and a "personal" style is crucial to serving your customers.

Some of you will resist this idea fiercely as your ego needs momentarily supersede your need to keep your job. Remember working for a company is not a right. It is a simple economic exchange where you supply labor or knowledge and the company pays you. It is a privilege the company grants you. To stay employed you have to give up some things in exchange.

Save your individual expression of freedom for *your* time.

A+ Work Habits

If you can manage it, checking in with your boss (as stated above) during the time before or after the work day are excellent times to casually solidify your relationship with the boss.

Where possible, imitate the working hours of your boss. He may start the day earlier and stay later than required. Follow his example.

> Man is man because he is free to operate within the framework of his destiny. He is free to deliberate, to make decisions, and to choose between alternatives.
> - Martin Luther Kling, Jr.

If your family commitments are such that you cannot be at the office outside of normal working hours, always be on time and start work right away, do not leave early or over-stay break time or lunch. Minimize your socializing while you are on the clock.

If you are not busy enough – leaving you time to socialize or be idle - ask the boss for more to do. Many employees are afraid to ask because they think the message conveyed is that a full time person is not needed for their regular work. More likely, the boss has tasks that need someone's attention and you are highlighting that you are willing to do more without being asked.

I can do that!

Be Proactive: Learn and Share

Continuously learn about your profession, the products you are working on, your customers. Join professional associations and attend the meetings and conferences that will increase your skills and knowledge. Choose which to attend based upon the topics and skills will most help your company, not just you. Once you have a good sense of the organization and its conferences, submit proposals to be an expert presenter on your subject matter.

> *James' company wasn't big on paying for training, so James found a way to get training with a contribution of his own and a contribution from the company. First, James would investigate to find areas where the company needed technical expertise. He then asked the company to pay his salary and not use any vacation days while he attended that training. That was the company's contribution. James contributed by paying for the training himself. The training increased his technical skills and as they became more relevant and necessary to the company, he became more valuable. He invested in himself and received a huge benefit: in two years James doubled his salary.*

Willingly share your expertise. This helps you build your visibility while connecting you with more people. Offer to attend trade shows and conduct training classes for attendees. Create and produce webinars to educate customers about your products. Participate in teleconferences with geographically diverse colleagues.

Keep in touch with the people you meet via all of these connections: You may want their expertise someday or leverage the relationship to help you in the future. Be present, visible and active. Thus, you will be more readily recognized and people will be more willing to take your call, answer your email and help you out.

Tip: Learn how to create powerful presentation slides that are more picture than words. Do not be one of those presenters who commit death by PowerPoint!

Share your achievements in articles and blogs as "best practices" so that others in your organization can imitate them, improve on them and continue to enhance your organization's effectiveness.

Volunteer to present proposals or product updates, especially if it gets you in front of decision-makers and people from other parts of the organization that may not be aware of your expertise and experience. Volunteer to lead or organize these meetings.

Be Part of the Team

As simple as the items below are, they send powerful messages that you are part of the tribe, you want to belong, you have pride in where you work and you want to help the company work together as a team.

- Attend company social events

- Help decorate for company parties

- Play the games at the company picnics to get to know your co-workers and their families

- Promote company charity events

- Participate in morale building initiatives like nominating someone for Employee of the Month or "Wear all one color Day"

- Post the company newsletter on your door/cube wall

- Go to the birthday lunches

- Wear your company's logo shirt on Fridays

> *Your ideas:*

If your boss is not the person who hired you

In this circumstance, you have to start from the ground up. Recognize that the key factors that you impressed upon the person who made the decision to hire you are gone. Find a way to make sure that your current boss is aware of your skill set and the experience that prompted your hiring in the first place.

Ask for a meeting with any new boss to:

- Review your role
- Reassess what you do for the company to ensure your role matches your skills
- Volunteer to do more and ask how you can best help her

The goal of the conversation is to help your boss see your value and how you can contribute to making her job easier.

Here is a sample dialogue:

You: Thanks for seeing me. I'm interested in us working together as effectively as possible.

Boss: Me too. Why don't we start with what you're currently working on…

You: Well, I have these three projects….(*report the status and progress of each, provide a bulleted outline of them in hard copy.*) Is there anything else about those you'd like to know?

Boss: Not right now. I'm sure we'll have other opportunities to fill in any gaps.

You: Sure. Some of the other things I've done include that municipal project last year. The new process map I provided helped eliminate a lot of redundancy and saved us a bundle. There was also the grant proposal submitted to the LA County – I had a big part in outlining the cost saving steps that got us the grant. I'm also doing a small project right now for the maintenance department – helping them analyze their overruns. I've already made some recommendations to get their inventory under control

Boss: Great. Sounds like you're pretty good at interpreting complex data and coming up with solutions.

You: I am and I enjoy it, so much in fact, I'm always willing to take these kinds of projects on, so let me know when something like this comes up. I'll be happy to pitch in.

(…and so on…)

Finish the conversation this way:

You: I really appreciate the opportunity to lay this out for you, let you know how my skills can be put to work. One thing I'll always make an effort to do is keep you informed of the results we're getting and how we can build on those. I'll also be taking responsibility to ask you regularly how I can do a better job for you. Thanks again.

Notice the emphasis was to provide your boss with *results* and *ideas* about how your skills helped the organization, not just stories of how wonderful you are. Be sure you understand the distinction so you do not come off as self-serving, but rather as helpful and valuable. You also laid the foundation for future conversations and their content: How to help *her* not you.

An example of changing responsibilities may illuminate this point. Gina was hired to research and document medical records for a Fortune 500 firm. Her background included writing technical documents and a Master's degree in Public Health. It was a perfect match for about 3 years. However, the company lost the contract under which she was paid. Because she had told her boss that she really enjoyed working with database information, he helped her find a job on a different contract that required someone to be able read, understand and interpret data.

If your boss is not really your target

In some employment situations, your direct supervisor may not be the person to which you have to direct your efforts. Consider if your boss is retiring or up for promotion outside of your department or looking for a job outside the company. These bosses may have no influence on the decision to keep you employed.

Your objective is to determine who will be your next boss and direct your Marketing Me efforts to him or to impress your boss' supervisor with your value (if you have not done this already.) This can be tricky because you do not want to poison your relationship with your current boss as he may decide to remain with the company. If your relationship is solid and he really is moving on, let him know what you are doing. Otherwise, be careful, subtle and minimize your activities until just before he leaves.

If you believe you are smarter than the boss

This is dangerous territory. First be certain that you really *are* smarter. You may know more about certain things like computer technology, but he very likely knows more about your industry and the inner workings of your company. Do your research before you

Smarter than the average bear!

act. If you determine you do have a better grasp of the reality of your company's business, its strategy, its players and the industry, proceed as I have recommended and promote your value to him. Expand your activities to include others with decision-makers.

General Keep your Job Skills

While I have outlined how to start doing more to put your value solidly in front of your boss, the list that follows expands on these ideas. The concept here is to establish a relationship that mutually benefits you and your boss.

Read the list and evaluate yourself: How many of these can you confidently say are a part of your everyday work habits?

Attentiveness:
Catch your own errors before others do. Become aware of changes in the industry, marketplace and products of your company. Know important peoples' birthdays and send greetings.

Carefulness:
Do you have a tendency to think and plan carefully before acting? This helps with reducing the chance for costly errors and maintains a steady workflow.

Cooperation:
Willingness to effectively engage in interpersonal work situations is very important in the workplace. This includes people you might not like personally and yet must work with. It may include people who have clout with the higher-ups.

Creativity:
Have you heard of "thinking outside the box"? Employers want innovative people who bring a fresh perspective. Develop this skill. I recommend the book A Whack on the Side of the Head by Roger von Oech to spark your creativity.

Discipline:

This includes the ability to stay on task and complete projects without becoming distracted or bored. Being on time, not wasting company resources, like *other* people's time, exemplifies discipline. It also includes the ability to control your expressions of emotions.

Drive:
Businesses want employees who have high aspiration levels and work hard to achieve goals. Just letting your boss know you set goals and achieve them demonstrates drive. Most people *do not* do this.

Good attitude:
A good attitude goes a long way toward productivity. Do everything you can to project a positive, can-do attitude. It will get noticed. Good attitudes are predictors of whether someone will engage in productive work behaviors vs. poor job performance, honesty vs. theft.

Goodwill:
Goodwill is a tendency to believe others are well-intentioned. The challenge to this characteristic occurs when conflict arises. Be sure your conflict resolution skills are well-established.

Graciousness:
Graciousness is the implementation of socially adept behaviors. These include:
- Good table manners
- Polite conversation (no swearing,)
- Use of appropriate titles (Mr., Mrs., Sir, Ma'am,)
- Preventing public gaffs
- Politely and humbly apologizing if you make a mistake

Graciousness is such a rare quality it stands out – pleasingly – when it is displayed.

A year ago, several of Karen's co-workers from remote locations and she were together for training on the east coast. Their boss took all of them out to a nice restaurant for dinner. As her mother trained her to do, Karen wrote a thank you note and mailed it to her boss. The next time she saw him, he brought up the thank you note. He told her he had never gotten a hand written thank you note before and couldn't believe it. He expressed that he was very impressed.

Influence:

Influence includes a tendency to positively impact social situations by speaking your mind and becoming a group leader. Groups need strong leaders to guide the way and establish a culture. An interesting study of this skill is in the book <u>Influencer</u> by Patterson, et al.

Order:

"Where did I put that?"
Order is a tendency to be well-organized which helps you work without major distractions or roadblocks. The amount of time, productivity and revenue lost to disorganization is staggering. Be sure you are not contributing to company waste by disorder.

Safe work behaviors:

Employers want people who avoid work-related accidents and unnecessary risk-taking in the work environment. So, report hazardous situations before they cause harm and no not create or perpetuate any.

Savvy:

Savvy is "know how." This is not just job knowledge. It is knowledge of coworkers and the working environment. It includes a tendency to read other people's motives from carefully observed behavior. A Savvy worker uses information to guide their thinking and actions to maximize collaboration and team success.

Sociability:
Sociability is friendliness. How well you interact socially with coworkers affects how well you work with them. Balance sociability with likability: Do people like working with *you*?

Stability:
Stability is the tendency to maintain composure and rationality in stressful work situations, to recover from upsets and move to action.

Teamwork:
Teamwork is the ability to form a team, participate, and depart from it without burning bridges.

Vigor:
Vigor is the ability to maintain a rapid tempo and stay busy.

Summary

In this chapter, you learned to think of yourself as a very important contributor to the results of your organization. You were encouraged to act as if your value is incalculable to your boss and your company.

Far and away the best prize that life offers is the chance to work hard at work worth doing.
- Theodore Roosevelt

Next Chapter

In the next chapter, I help you characterize your target market - your boss - and uncover the best ways to communicate with him. I give you tips for intelligently presenting the value of your contributions.

ACTION

☐ Recognize that your Marketing Me endeavor takes a change in your perspective and your mindset: Be prepared to think and act differently even if you are uncomfortable at first.

☐ Act as if you are a keeper: Come early, stay late, attend company social events, etc.

☐ Set up a meeting with your boss if you do not already meet regularly and start building a relationship founded on mutual benefit: work at building maximum visibility of your value.

Marketing Me

Chapter Four

Step 2: Understand Your Marketing Me Target Market

In this chapter, I describe your target market and develop a plan to effectively communicate to that market.

Marketing Research and Your Job

Every well run business strives to know as much as it can about their customers in order to provide the services or products that they desire. In fact, corporations spend millions each year on market research determining if new products or services will be purchased and by whom. They also determine the best price.

They do this research because it is much cheaper to invest in market research than to produce a product/service and find out that no one wants to buy it. Market research establishes if there are buyers for a product/service.

The Boss is the Target Market

You have the advantage of already knowing who your target market is: Your Boss. He or she is the one person that you have to design your Marketing Me campaign around. So, the difficult part of a normal marketing campaign is done.

Study your boss. Take a snapshot of what exactly he expects from you. Observe him under various situations. How he deals with the other people. Soon enough, you will see a pattern. Then it's your move. You have to mold yourself to fit into this pattern to get maximum traction from him.
Sunil Nair, Business Consultant, quoted on LinkedIn

Know How your Boss Prefers to Communicate

People behave in predictable ways. By observing a few key behaviors, you can generally predict how someone likes to communicate and receive information. With that data, begin to hone how you interact with your boss. This next section help you learn to communicate and behave in manners similar to hers. You immediately build a bond.

> *Men acquire a particular quality by constantly acting in a particular way.*
> *Aristotle*

The Boss' Favorites

Who are the boss' favorites? Bosses are not immune to playing favorites. When choosing whom to lay off, bosses are likely to choose those they *least* like working with or those whose work is least valuable to his standing in the company. You may have already seen this where you work. Generally, people are shocked when the office slacker or suck-up sticks around and one of the harder workers is let go.

How did this person become the favorite? People like people who are like themselves. The smart employee observes the things his boss is interested in and invests time in learning something about those same things. Add the Marketing Me actions I advocate in this book to take this practice to the next level.

> ...just the facts, Ma'am...

Communication Styles

How does your boss like to get information? Is your boss the verbal type who wants to talk about problems? Does he prefer that you draft a memo outlining the problem and then review it together? Does he prefer email instead of face to face? Does she prefer that you keep her apprised at every step of the problem or simply asks that you bottom line the problem and how it was solved?

Some bosses want total control and therefore it is important to over-inform them in their preferred manner. Others prefer only the bullet points.

Whatever his or her communication style is, you ignore it at your own peril. By cross-communicating, either by style or delivery, you are putting your job at serious risk.

> Sixty percent of misunderstandings can be traced to poor listening.

How do you figure out what your boss' preferred communication and decision making styles are?

Communication Styles: A primer

It is generally accepted by experts who study communication that there are two major continuums for communication styles. They go by many names, and if your company has ever implemented communication styles training, you have probably been introduced to them by a particular set of names.

The major communication preferences are *generically* known as **Closed to Open Expression** (the horizontal continuum) and **High Assertive to Low Assertive** (the vertical continuum.) (See the chart near the end of this chapter for an illustration.)

No style preference is better or more valuable than any other. They all have strengths and applications in different situations.

> *A good listener is not only popular everywhere, but after a while he knows something.*
> *Wilson Mizner, American playwright*

Closed to Open Expression Continuum

This continuum of communication preference, Closed to Open, indicates whether you are more likely to communicate one-on-one or to groups. It also indicates whether you prefer openly expressive communication (lots of gestures and voice inflection) or more constrained expression of thoughts and ideas. It is also a sign of

©2009 by Douglas J. Wolf

whether you are more energized by being with people (Opens) or by being with one person or alone (Closeds.)

Key indicators of Open VS Closed Expression

Closeds prefer one-on-one conversations, tend to stand at the fringe of conversation groups, speak up at the end of a group discussion, and generally do not interrupt. They are more likely to put their thoughts in writing and thoroughly report information. Their gestures and facial expressions are smaller, more limited and may be hard to read.

Opens prefer lively interactions and to be included in most any

conversation. They initiate discussions, even with strangers, interrupt to express a viewpoint and tend to speak spontaneously. They find instant messaging irresistible because they enjoy improvising and expressing what they are thinking on the spot. They can be terse or incomplete in their writing, preferring to converse face-to-face where they have the ability to "read" the person they are interacting with. Their gestures are large and their emotions are obvious and on the surface.

Open or Closed? Neither!

No one is all Closed or all Open: the difference between the two descriptions is gray – a range or continuum – not a line or specific simple delineation. The indicators are not always obvious. Closeds can be very open, expressive and talkative once they get to know you well. Many actors are Closed but they can act like Opens. Opens can become uncommunicative under stress or when they feel ostracized.

Tip: Deliver good news to your boss in writing so it is documented, and deliver bad news verbally.

Careful observation of your co-workers and boss' behaviors will improve your ability to identify these tendencies. Remember, these are tendencies and not written in stone. You will never be able to predict every time how someone will respond: People shift under extraordinary circumstances.

Collect clues by observing your boss' habits to discern his communication preferences. Which end of the continuum is he closer to? Do this for two-three weeks (or interact with him at least ten times.) Then you can imitate your boss' preferences and act more like him.

For instance, if your boss tends to send emails more than he picks up the phone, you can probably assume that he is more Closed.

However, that is not your only clue. Ask yourself:
- Does he speak more slowly or in a measured manner than others?
- Are his facial expressions neutral or flat? (Closed)
- Or are they more obvious: happy, frustrated, or amused? (Open)
- Does he explain things in detail (Closed) or prefer to provide generalities? (Open)

High Assertive to Low Assertive Continuum

Once you assess the Closed/Open preference of your boss, the next distinction to make is her preferred means of presenting information.

Answer these questions to assess her place on the High/Low Assertiveness continuum:
- Does your boss tell people what to do, think or feel?
- Or is she more likely to ask questions to determine what should be done, thought or felt?

This continuum is the assertiveness scale, from low assertiveness (where *asking* is the preferred behavior) to high assertiveness (*telling* is the preference.)

Watch how your boss delivers information. Does she fly by your desk and throw a command your way? Then she is on the High Assertive end. Does she send you an email and ask you to read an

> So shall it be written...so shall it be done.

attachment with some ideas and reply with your input? Likely, she is Low Assertive. In meetings, does she drive the agenda and make pronouncements? Likely she is High Assertive. However, even a Low

Assertive can take the floor and keep it by ignoring time limits or raised hands. So, include other clues about assertiveness in this assessment.

Key Indicators: High VS Low Assertive

Does she use words like "should" and "make" and "must"? Those are High Assertive words. Low assertives say "I think…" or "We might…" or "What about…" tending to cushion their ideas. High Assertives tend to issue orders or sound supremely confident even if they are stating opinions and not facts. A common phrase used by a Highly Assertive boss is, *"The fact is…"*

Dialog or Monolog?

Understanding "dialog" versus "monolog" aids your assessment of style. Low Assertives may take the floor and drone on with highly detailed information ignoring subtle (and maybe not so subtle) cues from audience members that they are bored to death. This is a strong indicator you are dealing with a Closed who is *not* Assertive, even though he is doing a good job of telling versus asking.

> Listen to others as you would have them listen to you.

What is the difference? There is no exchange, no dialog. Tellers, on the other hand, may seem to discourage a dialog but actually relish a good debate.

Exercise: Communication Matrix

Now, combine the two major indicators and determine: what are you dealing with when it comes to communicating with your boss?

For example, a person who is a combination of High Assertive + Closed Expression styles may seem terse, insensitive, even bordering on abusive. A person whose styles are Low Assertive + Closed Expression may appear indecisive and highly analytical. When someone's styles are a combination of High Assertive and Open Expression styles, they tend to be talkative and friendly, leaning toward light discussion and stories. Finally, a person whose styles tend toward Low Assertive and Open Expression will be personable, helpful and acquiescent.

Look at the chart on the next page and put an X where you think you boss falls on each of the two lines: one on the horizontal (High/Low Assertiveness) and one on the vertical (Open/Closed Expression). Next, do the same for you, using an O for your location.

Compare the two letters. The closer you are on either line to your Boss' X, the easier it will be for you to match his style on that aspect of communication styles. Conversely, the further apart you are, the more work it will be for you to match his style. Read that again – the more work *for you!* Do not expect your boss to flex or change. If he does, you are fortunate, and you probably were not aware of it…until now. Make communicating with him easier by also flexing.

> *Things do not change;*
> *we change.*
>
> *Henry David Thoreau*

Where is your Boss' Communication Style on this grid?
Where is yours?

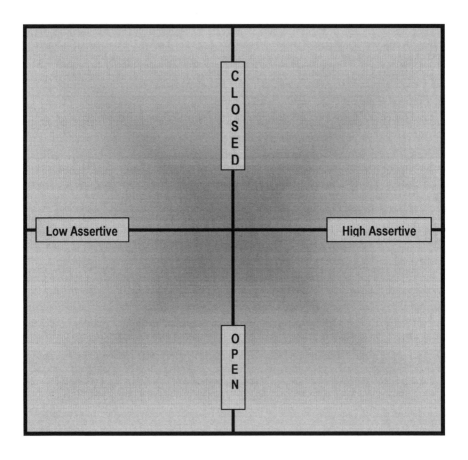

Nature has given to man one tongue, but two ears, that we may
hear from others twice as much as we speak.

Epictetus

How to Flex Your Style

If your boss is Open Expression:

- Use larger, more obvious gestures, both with your hand and face
- Readily state your opinions
- Smile, nod, or tilt your head when listening
- Choose to communicate face to face or on the phone instead of by email, if you have the option.
- Liberally use expressive adjectives and adverbs such as very, much, more, great, big, and tiny

If your Boss is Closed Expression:

- Speak to match his pace, which will usually be slower
- Choose email versus face to face communication
- Do not interrupt
- Keep your hand and facial gestures small and subtle

> Be swift to hear and slow to speak.

If your Boss is High Assertive:

- Do not take his terseness personally
- Listen for content and ask questions. Do not be put off by his direct delivery style
- Be concise when speaking and writing: Use headlines to give him the most salient points upfront
- Interject questions and comments with strength
- If you interrupt, do it with power
- Use direct words: Should, will, do, do not versus could, might, and try
- Skip the niceties and chitchat about your personal life or his. Get right down to business in any discussion. Exception: If you and he have met on the battlefield (golf, opposing sports' teams, etc.) be prepared to banter a bit about winning and losing

If your Boss is Low Assertive:

- Be prepared to ask questions, insert opinions, and solicit his opinion versus wait for answers or expect him to tell you what he is thinking
- Use cushioning or softening words/phrases (I think, what about, we might, could we) to present ideas
- Listen carefully before responding, even repeating or summarizing what you have heard if necessary
- Take time for a short chat about personal things such as family, pets and hobbies

Never overdo your imitation of style preferences, especially if you are on the opposite end of the spectrum from your boss. Your goal is to be you; just flex toward a middle ground that is more comfortable for your boss. Remember, people like to be around people they like.

Summary

In this chapter, I provided tools to determine the optimum way to communicate with your boss and told you how to use those tools.

Next Chapter

Chapter 5 provides a set of ideas and techniques to build your own performance review and make your boss' job even easier.

ACTION

- [ ] Carefully observe your boss to determine his communication style preferences. Take the next 2-3 weeks to do this.

- [ ] If necessary, slowly begin flexing your style to more closely match his, without being obvious or superficial

- [ ] Listen more carefully than you ever have in your life: you will appear involved and helpful

- [ ] Take mental notes on who seems to be the favorites in your boss's team and get to know them.

- [ ] If you previously avoided your boss's favorites out of personal dislike, then let go of your need to be comfortable around everyone right now. It is better for your future to be seen getting along with the favored players.

Marketing Me

Chapter Five

Step 3: Build Your Own Performance Review

In this chapter, I show you the best way to present yourself in day to day work and to excel in that crucial performance review with your boss.

The dreaded performance review. Supervisors hate doing them and employees hate getting them! They are time consuming, painful. Most people can not make the connection to how performance reviews directly impact revenue. Performance Review conversations that are supposed to be chock full of helpful feedback and motivation are usually short, non-specific and basically a waste of time.

Imagine being required to complete performance reviews for several employees, including a multi-page document with a long list of questions to answer and items to rank. Bosses procrastinate until Human Resources is jumping up and down in front of their desks demanding the reviews get done. Most bosses would rather concentrate on revenue producing activities.

Let's Get This Over With

For your boss, the prospect of an uncomfortable and non-productive conversation causes the actual performance review to be as brief and as non-confrontational as possible. Your boss just wants to check this grueling task off his list .

Unfortunately, the conversations typically go something like this:

> **Boss**: So, this year your performance review is pretty good. Here's your copy – you need to sign it at the bottom there. Any questions?
> **You**: Nope.
> **Boss**: Good. That's it.
> **You**: Thanks.

OR

> **Boss**: There are a couple of things here in your review that you probably want to look at. Here's your copy. You want to discuss any of this?
> **You**: Not especially.
> **Boss**: OK. Just sign it on the bottom there.
> **You**: OK
> **Boss**: Good. That's done for another year.

You can almost hear both of them saying, "Let's just get the darn thing signed and move on to something more important."

Make It Easier

If you make this dreadful task easier for your boss, you may receive an unexpected benefit: Your boss just might kiss the ground you walk on.

To write a good review requires collecting an employee's major accomplishments and, if indicated, mistakes. Most bosses do not track this information in any detail over the course of a year. So, when it comes time to write up examples of how an employee "Exhibits good work habits" or "Takes initiative" – the kinds of questions on every performance review – bosses do not have records of specific examples.

During the performance review conversation, bosses hem and haw, completely lacking any good or bad work examples. Sometimes they will throw out general statements about how they see your work going, but often they share minimum, vague impressions or perceptions, and end the meeting.

There it is again - the importance of managing your boss' perceptions of you and your work. Your Performance Review becomes a permanent record of his perceptions, and, up to now, you have been relying on his poor memory of your accomplishments to complete that significant document.

Building Your Performance Review allows you to change that. The best performance review is the one that you influence. So, help your boss compile it by giving him information about absolutely every accomplishment and bottom-line result you have impacted.

Greg supervised 17 people and dreaded the month of November when he had to complete all of their performance reviews. "It takes the entire month and oh, those awful meetings!" One October, Karolov took the initiative to send Greg a chronological summary of his projects for the previous 12 months, including copies of relevant emails from colleagues he had worked with praising his contributions. Greg was not only grateful, he asked Karolov to send a copy of his summary to 6 of Greg's other team members along with a cover note from Greg asking them to follow Karolov's example in preparation for their reviews. The following month, Greg assigned Karolov other supervisory responsibilities, telling him that his initiative had made the difference between Karolov getting those plumb assignments versus other team members.

Build Your Review

I assume you have not been doing anything in this area. Today your task is to begin that comprehensive compilation, like Karalov did and build your annual review.

Step One: meticulously track your accomplishments

- START today!
- In a spreadsheet, (a sample is on my website) record what you complete or achieve, even the small things, like getting a monthly report in on time
- Note the date and time, especially if time was an important part of the deadline
- Include anything notable, such as that the accuracy of your report was mentioned by the District Manager, the project came in on

©2009 by Douglas J. Wolf

budget or your boss complimented you that it was "better than everyone else's". These memory joggers will help you and your boss more completely recall the events.

• Note whether you have a related email or IM (See below and remember to save them!) that corroborates these notes. Include the sender's name, date, and the folder it is saved in. Therefore, you can find it when it is time to submit this log and emails to your boss.

Step Two: collect accolades and testimonials

Solicit and collect testimonials (brief emails) from people with whom you work relating your expertise and contributions.

Here are some sample ways to ask for these:

> **You**: Here's the report you asked for, a day ahead of the due date!
> **Co-worker**: Great! Thanks. That makes it easier for me to finish my part of this monster…
> **You:** Yeah, I figured that would be helpful. So, I'd appreciate it if you'd do something for me?
> **Co-worker:** Ok…
> **You:** If I send you some text in an email about how I got this in on time, would you copy and paste it into an email to my boss today? **APPLAUSE**
> **Co-worker:** I guess I could do that…
> **You:** Thanks. I'll get it to you in the next few minutes so you can send it right away.
> **Co-worker:** OK. Not a problem.
> **You**: Thanks again.

OR

> **You:** Hey, Gary. Here's the specs you need. Are you waiting on me for anything else?
> **Co-worker:** Thanks. No, I'm pretty sure you've gotten all your stuff to me already.
> **You:** So, we're all good.

Co-worker: Yep. And you're the only one who's done that. There's a lot of information still out there…

You: Huh. Sorry to hear that…wouldn't want this project to get derailed. Hey, I have a favor to ask.

Co-worker: Sure. What's up?

You: Since this project is such a big deal to my boss, I'd appreciate it if you'd let him know I got all my stuff into you on time. I could write a short email and send it to you so you can copy and paste it into a message to him today. Would that work for you?

Co-worker: If you make it that easy, sure. No problem.

You: And copy me in, too, so I know when he gets it.

Co-worker: Sure.

You: Great. I really appreciate that.

Notice that you ask the person to get this done *today*, and that you provide the information he requires. The result is you make sending the testimonial nearly effortless. Get in the habit of asking coworkers to endorse your good work.

> *Tip:* Always ask for these testimonials at the time you deliver your work product. Don't wait! Don't let them put you off, either! Ask them, politely, to do it now, today.

Endorsements are especially valuable if they come from a variety of people, including your boss. It is similar to collecting recommendations when you are looking for a job. But, for Marketing Me, you are constantly collecting statements that support your performance review versus your resume. Obviously, if you do lose your job, these supportive statements will be incredibly valuable as references.

"It's not easy to ask people for testimonials…"

Why do we find it hard to ask people to sing our praise or give us commendation when we have done good work? The most common reason is that we are afraid others will say no. Of course they can! But, most reasonable people are willing to help and they are more likely to do it if you <u>make it easy</u> for them.

©2009 by Douglas J. Wolf

Another reason we do not ask for testimonials is our doubt that what we did actually deserves praise. Really, we are just doing what we are supposed to do: Getting things done on time, under budget, up to spec, etc.

True, it is not important to get accolades for everything you do. It is vital to get them for work you do that is valuable to the company and your boss. Make sure what you are contributing is what your company and/or your boss wants and needs, in addition to getting things in on time or under budget or without mistakes. When you complete those above and beyond activities, ask for endorsements and testimonials. You demonstrate that you know what is important and that you are doing those things regularly and well.

> *A wise man will make more opportunities than he finds.*
> *Sir Francis Bacon*

If you request testimonials and people refuse or they equivocate, saying things like, "Well, I really don't have time…" or "I'm not sure that's such a good idea …" then you have a problem. Either you are not considered valuable to this person, you have managed to make it hard for them to endorse you or your work, or they have not told you they are not satisfied with your work. It is time for an honest, heart to heart conversation about your performance for this person. You must initiate it because *you* need to uncover how you are not meeting expectations. Only then can you improve and make it more likely you keep your job. See Step Three on the next page about asking for feedback to learn more about having these kinds of conversations.

> Of note: When you leave most companies, the only information that HR or your boss can safely provide to those seeking references are your employment dates, closing salary and, if they are really brave, whether or not they would rehire you.

Why companies do not offer more than that basic information is because of unfortunate lawsuits regarding information offered during reference conversations. People who did not get jobs found out the reason was a "bad" reference so they sued the source of the reference, usually a former employer, and won damages. So now the only information many former employers will provide is objective data.

You, however, can collect your accolades and use them if you have to get a different job.

Step Three: Ask for Feedback

Ask for performance feedback frequently and consistently. Find out what your boss thinks you need to do better or do more of by simply asking.

> **You:** So, that's the current status of our project. I'd like to ask you for some feedback. What one thing can I do to be a better employee for you?"

The first few times you ask, you may get no answer.

> **You**: What one thing can I do to be a better employee for you?
> **Boss**: You're doing great. Just keep it up.
> **You**: Thank you

Always respond with, "Thank you." That is it. Do not pursue the question further at this point. You will have opportunities in the future to ask for feedback in this manner.

You boss *may* make an odd remark such as, "Well, it'd help me if you could figure out how to make it stop raining so we can finally fix the roof!"

While seemingly offhanded, these remarks have some importance to your boss either because they are urgent or seemingly unsolvable. Again, say thanks, and move on. If you do happen to come up with a solution to the aforementioned problem, offer it. But recall that your goal is to manage your boss' perception of you and build your Performance Review with the record of improvements you make.

The key to asking for feedback is that if you are given some advice or a request for change you must act on it. Do not neglect it or dismiss it as unimportant. You are setting a precedent and the one you want to establish is that you listen and you respond. Woe to you if you get advice and you ignore it! Overcoming the perception that you asked for and then disregarded a suggestion for improvement is nearly impossible. You will not get another valuable piece of feedback nor the opportunity to make up for the one you ignored.

> *Feedback is a gift.*
> *Accept it graciously*
> *with reverence for the*
> *intention of the giver.*

People who give honest feedback are rare and valuable. Cultivate them and you will receive many helpful suggestions over the years. Reciprocity exists because the other person feels rewarded for having helped you; a simple yet worthwhile gift you give in return.

In about 30 days, when you have another meeting with your boss, ask again.

> **You**: "What one thing can I do to be a better employee for you?"

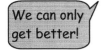

Notice that the question is about helping your boss by being a better employee, not about making you look good. And it is the *same* question. Repeat your gracious "Thank you" in response and act on the suggestion.

Keep Asking

Eventually, you will get some feedback you can act upon. Respond with, "Thank you." Take notes if you need to. Record what your boss said, the date, and put a tickler in your calendar to follow up to stay organized as described in Chapter 9.

If you actually do get a piece of advice or suggestion for improvement you MUST act on it. For the first few times you ask this, the suggestions re most likely going to be minor changes in your behavior or things you can easily do. Bosses often say things like:

> **Boss**: Could you send me some ideas about the Bronx proposal? There are a few areas in it that are a bit thin.
> **You**: Of course, right away.

Why not go out on a limb? Isn't that where the fruit is?
Frank Scully, Author

OR

> **You**: What one thing can I do to be a better employee for you?
> **Boss**: You're just going to keep asking that aren't you?"
> **You**: Yes, I am. I want to continue doing the very best I can.
> OR
> **You:** Well, yes, because doing what you need me to do is important to both of us.

OR

> **Boss**: I haven't thought of anything since the last time you asked.
> **You**: Well, I'm always open to improving so if you do think of anything, let me know.

OR

> **Boss**: Well, there is one thing…it'd be helpful if your monthly report had a bit more information about how your mail campaigns go. You've been putting in the number of pieces sent. What about the number of mailings that have been returned or were undeliverable?

Your response is,
> **You**: Thank you. I'll get right on that

You can always add statement of action:

> **You**: I'll make that change.
> **You**: That'll take me a few days but I'll get it done.
> **You**: I can do that. Is there a specific day you'd like it done?

Ask again every 30-90 days. When you get feedback you can act on, wait to ask again until after you have gotten some results or feel comfortable that you have made the changes. Do not ask again too soon because if you get another piece of actionable feedback, you may get overwhelmed with things to change.

> *Tip: Be prepared to take notes when you ask for feedback, but don't get too focused on recording every word. Listen first, record later.*

If you do not understand what your boss is asking you to change, repeat what he said, and ask for clarification. Do not guess. Do not assume you know. If you respond inaccurately on incorrectly to the feedback, you now have an error to clean up.

> **You**: What one thing can I do to be a better employee for you?
> **Boss**: Well, you're not as involved in the Revenue meeting as I'd like.
> **You**: You'd like me to be more involved in the revenue meeting. I'm not exactly sure what you'd like to see me do. Could you tell me more?

OR

> **You**: What one thing can I do to be a better employee for you?
> **Boss**: "Seems to me I told you something about this a week ago – don't you remember?
> **You**: Sorry, I guess I didn't catch it – or I'm not remembering right now. Remind me?

This exchange illustrates how easy it could be to get defensive, especially since this boss is stating his feedback indirectly or vaguely. It would be normal to feel a bit annoyed. It is important to managing his perception that you not respond with irritation or impatience. Stay open to the feedback, hard as that may be. You will get better over time – and so will he. Be *curious* about exactly what he is saying so you can respond accurately and immediately.

> *Experience is not what happens to you but what you make of what happens to you.*
>
> *Aldous Huxley*

Do not get Defensive

Here are a few examples of how you DO NOT want to react:

> **You**: What one thing can I do to be a better employee for you?
> **Boss**: I'm still not happy with your results from last quarter. What are you going to do about it?
> **You**: Geez, get off it already, will ya? We're making it up this quarter.

Better response:

> **You**: Thank you. As you and I agreed, I'm making up for it this quarter. I sent an update yesterday. Would you like to go over it?

> **You**: What one thing can I do to be a better employee for you?
> **Boss**: "How about getting your team to finish that design project on time this time?

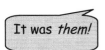

> **You**: You know that last project got derailed by the artistic team – not us! Heck, if I could get them to step up we'd all be happier.

Better response:

> **You**: Thank you. I've set up a series of project meetings with the artistic team so we don't get surprised if they get behind like last time. So far, we're all on schedule and everyone is checking in on each other more. Do you have any other suggestions for working with them?

Boss: Sounds good. Let me know if anything starts lagging. I don't want to be surprised again, either."
You: "Sure. Thanks again.

Remember, you asked for the feedback: You have to be willing to accept it.

Feedback is the breakfast of champions.
Rick Tate, Speaker

Now what do I do?!?

Rarely, you may get feedback to which you are unsure of how to respond. Sometimes what the boss asks for seems impossible or irrelevant. In both cases, it is important to:
- Listen carefully
- Say thank you
- Add that you will consider what was said

Take the advice or feedback to a trusted colleague, mentor, coach, or friend. Request their help to get perspective and help you choose a course of action.

Sometimes your boss can be really off the mark. This is rare but it does happen. When your boss gives you feedback that is confusing or appears inaccurate, you may not be able to come up with a reasonable change or response. Return to your Boss and tell him that you are unsure how to respond and would like more information or specific advice on the problem he mentioned.

Reapproaching your boss is a strategy that often produces positive outcomes. Usually, he will have a better response and you can act on that idea. By chance if he repeats the request or becomes angry, I recommend that you seek coaching. See the Resources section on my website to be referred to a Marketing Me coach. Working with an angry or unreasonable boss requires finesse, excellent communication, and conflict resolution skills.

Step Four: Follow up on Feedback

After obtaining feedback, give yourself at least 30 days to work on it. Take 90 days if the change is a complex or challenging.

Then meet with your boss and say,

> **You**: Remember when you shared with me that I needed to work on XXX? How am I doing on that?

Record what your boss says. If he says you still need to work on it, ask him for specifics (if he does not offer.) Use your calendar to continue your follow up, like this:
- ask again in 90 days, and ask again for specifics
- If he declares that the improvement is noticeable and adequate, thank him.
- In 30 days, ask the initial question again. ("What can I do to be a better employee for you?")
- Repeat this cycle to remind your boss that you seek to continue improving your performance

Miguel asked his boss for feedback, as we recommend in this chapter. His boss, after hemming and hawing a bit said, "Miguel, you have a way of telling people what you think that makes them feel attacked by you, like you're judging them or something. Haven't you noticed how they get defensive?" Miguel, initially taken aback, recovered and replied, "Thank you for telling me. I have noticed but didn't think it was something I was doing. I'll be more aware of that." Because Miguel was absolutely clueless as to what he was saying or doing that caused the reaction in others described by his boss, he sought out a coach. Then he tried a different tone of voice and words to express his thoughts in meetings, even asking questions instead of just telling people his thoughts. There was an immediate change in how others responded. In 30 days, Miguel again asked his boss for feedback. His boss, smiling broadly, said, "Miguel, whatever it is that your coach is telling you to do, keep it up! People are actually coming up to me to tell me how you've changed and how much easier it is to work with you." Miguel was relieved and grateful, and eventually received an assignment to work on a very important selection committee.

How this Feedback Helps You

Why do I prescribe feedback seeking?

It is a rare and wonderful opportunity to receive ideas on how you can grow, be given the opportunity to act on them and get additional feedback on how well you do.

Feedback seeking:
- Builds the impression that you want to improve and that you respect your boss' assessment of what you need to work on.
- Allows you to collect valuable information on what is important to your boss about your performance and your job.
- Gives your boss the opportunity to tell you what to improve. They often do not know how to do it well.
- Saves annoying your boss because he has not found a time or manner by which to share his feedback.
- Establishes a consistent, positive forum for these kinds of conversations. Recall that the Marketing Me mindset is focused on a proactive, positive approach to promoting your value.
- Demonstrates a specific positive change you have made that your boss had influence over. That makes him feel better about the kind of management job he is doing. He can tell *his* boss the impact he is having on his team.

  We're in this together....
- Gives your boss the opportunity to help you improve. This is what most bosses want to do and many are not able to find the time to do so.

Through practicing the Marketing Me technique of seeking feedback, you improve and develop your skills, especially those all important interpersonal skills You receive specific feedback and act on it, demonstrating your willingness to contribute positively to your company. All of your improvements are recorded and build your Performance Review.

Closing Thoughts on Step Four

Recall the emotional back account concept from Stephen Covey's book, The Seven Habits of Highly Effective People.

Asking for feedback is a sincere way to build a relationship with your boss and is another means to help him know, like and trust you.

> *The only job security you have today is your commitment to continuous improvement.*
>
> *Ken Blanchard, Author*

Step Five: Build Your Review

When it is time for your performance review, tell your boss you have catalogued your accomplishments over the year. Offer to provide him a copy of the document prior to the review due date. Alternately, set up a time to meet when you can both go over the information.

Be sure the document you provide is top notch:
- Proofread all documents for grammar, spelling and punctuation
- Check that your information is presented is in a logical format, such as chronologically or by project
- Include samples of your work such as spreadsheets, documents, presentations, (slides or handouts), articles, etc.

What if my company does not have a formal Performance Review process?

Marketing Me success revolves around you taking the initiative here. Without a documented performance review, how would anyone other than you know you have added value? If you wanted to change jobs within the company or pursue a promotion you need a positive tool to help market you. Without a formal document, no future boss will have a record of your contributions and achievements. You want a paper trail on your performance.

I'm a Keeper... says so right there.

Track your contributions, accomplishments and achievements to build your own review. This is a key Marketing Me concept.

Never assume anyone knows you are doing a great job.

Take it to the next step. Posted on my website in the Resources section is a template document you can fill in with your tracked activities. Present this document to your boss at regular intervals or after you have just completed a major project. Keep in mind, recording your activities has a two-fold purpose:

1. It demonstrates your ongoing value
2. It makes it easier for your boss to complete your review and justify keeping you.

> *The future depends on what we do in the present.*
> *Mahatma Gandhi*

Self-Reviews

Some companies require employees to fill out a self-review, a document offering your perspective on your progress and achievements. Your Marketing Me compilation of accomplishments is well-suited to help you complete a self-review. Use these sample sentences and phrases to complete a self-review:

1. I completed Project x on time and within budget on June 13th. The team I worked with said this about this achievement: (insert testimonial)
2. On May 1st, I participated in a strategic project meeting with 28 other managers and led the sub-team that created the newest website initiative that gathers customer feedback on Product B.
3. The Product B feedback portal was posted Sept 1st to our website, a month ahead of the project schedule. This was due primarily to the template I created that saved the team having to consult with IT to build it.
4. My boss and I met twice per month during the last quarter (list dates) during which I kept him in the loop on several production issues. In particular, I brought to his attention the bottleneck on line 61 and a solution that he took to his boss. It was implemented Jan 31st and improved throughput by 15% since that date.

Wow! I did all that?

The more specific your self-review statements, the more compelling your accomplishments. Include dates, revenue impact, timelines, and percents of increase. Describe he impact you had, not only your accomplishments.

Creating your review may have an unexpected consequence: You may recognize that your job description does not match what you are actually doing day-to-day. How fortunate for you!

You now have the opportunity to rewrite your job description and submit it as part of this review. This is another example of proactively helping your boss do his job better and consequently look good to his colleagues. Grab a copy of your current job description – if one exists – or the one you got when you got this job, and begin revising it. There are templates on my website in the Resources section to help you get started`.

> *Observation leads to evaluation which is a necessary step to transformation.*
>
> *Roger Crawford, Speaker*

To Get Started

One easy way to get started on a new job description is to ask, "What do I *really* do?"

- Make a list and remember to look back at your recorded accomplishments.
- Think about what you do everyday, every week, once a month, once a quarter, once a year. Include it all.
- Make special note of responsibilities you have added since you were hired and since your last review.
- If you have a Human Resources department, ask them to review your revised job description to ensure it complies with your company's format for this document.

You have the responsibility to keep your boss informed. This technique helps you fulfill that responsibility.

Last Step

When it is time to submit the self-review, send your boss *your* version. If your company has no formal process or form, send him the template from my website with your information filled in. Insert or attach the email testimonials you have collected. Do this a few days before you have the performance review conversation with your boss so he has time to review it.

Then both you and your boss can enjoy your Performance Review!

Performance Review Discoveries

If your day-to-day role has changed substantially, you may discover as part of this process that what you are doing now does not lead to accomplishing your goals. Or you may learn you have taken on responsibilities or tasks that you do not enjoy. There is a phrase in most job descriptions that declares: "Other duties as assigned." In project management language, getting "other duties" is called "scope creep:" In other words, the parameters of your role have changed.

Ask yourself:
- Is this what I want to be doing right now?
- Am I OK with doing this for the next 3 years? 5 years?
- Am I achieving my *professional* goals? All of them or some?
- Is this role helping me achieve my *personal* goals?
- Am I actually getting ahead compared to where I was a year ago?
- Am I stagnant or just filling time?

If your current role and tasks associated with it support your professional goals, make that clear in the documentation you prepare for your Performance Review. You may want to use them as headers to sort your responsibilities. That format helps make the list more readable.

Have you clearly defined your goals so you can determine whether your job role and responsibilities are helping you achieve them?

If your responsibilities are NOT moving you toward your goals, decide if you want to ask for different responsibilities or look for another position, either inside your current company or with a new company. I recommend you engage a career coach to help you with this decision. An excellent coach can be reached by contacting Rebecca@RebeccaEverett.com

Summary

This chapter recommended you take a series of actions to establish yourself as a valuable contributor. I emphasized the importance of making your boss' job easier. This is Marketing Me's central thread. If you have started implementing my recommendations, you have momentum that will carry you forward into the following chapters.

Carefully review and implement my recommendations in this chapter. Reread it many times to integrate the concepts into your daily Marketing Me campaign.

Next Chapter

Chapter 6 is another stage in the implementation of your Marketing Me plan in which you take small but consistent actions to increase your visibility and esteem.

ACTION

- ☐ Start tracking your accomplishments TODAY if you are not already
- ☐ Collect testimonials and recommendations to support your record of accomplishments
- ☐ Assume responsibility for building your performance review to make your boss' job easier
- ☐ Ask for feedback so you continuously improve and manage your boss' perception of your willingness to develop your skills

Chapter Six:

Step 4: Campaign for Yourself - Micro Marketing Me Activities

In this chapter I show you how to begin your marketing campaign, implementing small Marketing Me suggestions that change the way your boss and co-workers perceive you.

A Personal Marketing Message

In social situations you are often asked. "What do you do?" The question is usually social banter seeking common ground. However, sometimes people ask because the question is business related. They are curious about what it is you do for a living. Their question is more likely to be business related when you are at a networking event, a business meeting, a convention or a professional conference. The answer you want to give is your personal well-crafted, brief Marketing Me message.

One form of a personal marketing message is an *elevator speech*, used when you are in an elevator and someone asks you: "What do you do?" Most elevator rides are short with little time to explain in detail what you do.

Imagine riding in an elevator with the CEO of your company. He asks, "What do you do for our company?"

> *Be a Lion for your own cause.*
> *Scottish proverb*

You want to state a brief, compelling description of your role and results you have achieved.

Having a clear, compelling Marketing Me message will accomplish two things:

1. He will be impressed with your confidence
2. He will definitely remember you

Imagine, in that elevator ride with the CEO, that your personal marketing message is "I work on the 2nd floor."

The conversation quickly ends and you miss the opportunity to impress this decision maker.

If I met you at a networking event today and asked what you do, what would your answer be? Would it be:

> "I am an accountant."
> "I am in charge of shipping."
> "I manage a sales team"

The answers above may be factually correct, but they do not open up a conversation.

A better response will have two components:

1. A brief description of what you *do* for your company
2. A brief statement of a specific *result* you have achieved, a result that demonstrates your excellence and competence

People hearing this Marketing Me message will be impressed with your confidence and remember you and your results.

Suppose you collect receivables at your company and that elevator ride with the CEO occurs.

Current personal marketing message:

> **CEO**: Good morning, do you work for XYZ?
> **You**: Good morning, yes, I do work here.
> **CEO**: And what is it you do for the company?
> **You**: I am in the credit and collections department.
> **CEO**: Nice weather we're having….

Coulda, woulda, shoulda…

New Personal Marketing Message

> **CEO**: Good morning, do you work for XYZ?
> **You**: Good morning, yes, I do work here.
> **CEO:** And what is it you do for our company?
> **You:** I save our company thousands of dollars a year.
> **CEO**: Really? And just how do you do that?
> **You:** I work in the collections department and make sure our customers pay their bills in a timely fashion, reducing our capital costs.
> **CEO**: Terrific! I forgot to ask your name.
> **You:** It's Benny, Benny Benicio.
> **CEO:** Nice to meet you, Benny. Do you have your card with you? I am always looking for people in our company who help us improve things.

The difference in the messages and their impact is dramatic. The reason the new personal marketing message works is that you are stating a benefit that the CEO is interested in and you lead him to ask a second question about you. You begin the process of getting the CEO to know, like and trust you. This does not mean that he will call you the next day and make you head of accounting, but the concept applies. It is not an exaggeration to say that this kind of single interaction, if handled properly, could change your career.

Here is a second example:

Current personal marketing message

> **CEO**: Good morning, do you work for XYZ?
> **You**: Good morning, yes I do work here.
> **CEO**: And what is it you do for the company?
> **You**: I manage the customer service team.
> **CEO**: I see. I hope we don't get too many complaints....

New personal marketing message

> **CEO**: Good morning, do you work for XYZ?
> **You**: Good morning to you, yes I do work here.
> **CEO**: And what is it you do for our company?
> **You**: I generate thousands of dollars in revenue for our company.

CEO: Really? Are you on my sales team?

You: Actually, I manage our customer service department and I make sure that every time a customer calls with a problem, my staff handles it with courtesy and the problem is resolved to the customer's satisfaction.

CEO: Really? So you're the one responsible for our customer survey satisfaction rating going up last year?

You: Why, yes, I am.

CEO: Well, congratulations. I really commend you for your efforts. Who is your supervisor? I'd like to make sure he knows you and I've talked and how much I appreciate your work.

You: Thank you.

While it may not often occur that you are alone in the elevator with the CEO of your company, you want to be prepared! Craft your Marketing Me message *as if* that situation will occur. Be ready. You will impress anyone with a Marketing Me that is created to impress the CEO. You will have the opportunity to use the message you create in many other situations.

> *Lack of something to feel important about is almost the greatest tragedy a man may have*
> *Arthur E. Morgan, TVA Engineer*

Create Your Personal Marketing Message

Step One

Think about the job you do and how you would describe it to someone as it *benefits* the company. After all, if the company is not benefiting from what you do, they will not need you for very long. Try out your personal marketing message with a trusted friend or co-worker. If the initial answer you give does not compel them to ask, "How do you do that?" you have not hit your target. Keep refining your message until you hit that mark.

Step Two

After you are satisfied with your personal marketing message, practice! Say it to enough people as many times as you need until it comfortably rolls off your tongue. Practice in front of a mirror and force yourself to look directly in your own eyes. You will know you have mastered your personal marketing message when saying it feels the same as saying your name.

Still, the first few times you do this in response to that question from others it will feel awkward and faked, like you are reading a script. This is normal. The truth is, you are already using a scripted personal marketing message that is probably very mediocre and may be hurting your career or at least not helping it at all. Better to have your personal marketing message honed so that when you are asked the question "What do you do?" your answer clearly states your value and makes you memorable.

Dress Up your Email Signature

The vast majority of business communications take place today via email. It may be the only way some people communicate with you. You want your email message signature to contain several vital pieces of information that help promote you and your value:
1. Your job title
2. Your photo
3. Your tag line
4. Your signature

Most people use a version of Microsoft Outlook which can be modified to include the items on this list. Use HTML email formats that allow for pictures and special fonts for your digital signature.

Your Job Title

Always include a job title and add your division or location to make finding you easier.

Your Photo

Use a current picture, framing your head. The resulting photo must look good at 1 inch by 1 inch dimension. Use a photo in which you appear pleasant and friendly. If you have several acceptable photos in your files, change your photo from time to time.

> *Tip:* Don't use a photo from your cell phone-most do not have the resolution to produce a sharp picture. Use a digital camera with excellent resolution. You deserve to look your best.

Your Tag Line

A tag line is another form of your Marketing Me personal marketing message. If your company does not have an official tag line for email, you have the opportunity to create one that succinctly describes what you do and includes a benefit to the company.

For someone in collections, a tag line might be:
"Turning receivables into cash"

For a sales person:
"Call me for the perfect carpet solution"

The first tag line represents an internal email signature sent others in your company. The second is targeted to prospects or customers, but may also be used internally. You may want to create several email signatures with different tag lines for different recipients.

Other examples:

> Resistance is futile.

- Moving Products to Production (Warehouse)
- Connecting People to Potential (Human Resources)
- Turning Ideas into Results (Sales)
- Getting Data in your Hands (IT)
- Connecting Ideas to Actions (Executive Coach)
- So You Can Sleep At Night (Security)

Some examples of familiar company taglines are:

- Fly The Friendly Skies   (*United Airlines*)
- Absolutely, Positively Overnight (*Fedex*)
- Innovating for a Safer World   (*BAE Systems*)
- Strength On Your Side   (*General Dynamics*)
- High Performance. Delivered   (*Accenture*)

Use these as inspiration for creating your own Marketing Me tag line.

One of our clients liked this idea but could not come up with a suitable tag line. She never sends email outside of her company. Her job consists of generating multiple report types from raw data for a variety of managers - not an easy role to describe concisely. We suggested the tag line "Turning data into information" which perfectly conveyed her role. The folks who work with her understand what the tag line means. Also, when someone sees that tagline the first time, the natural question is, how does she do that?

Your Signature

In this section, I present the steps to create a signature file in Microsoft Outlook. Outlook 2007 uses Word for editing email, allowing you to choose from many fonts and styles. Outlook 2003 also uses various fonts to enhance your signature, but it does not use Word.

One type of signature is the Holographic signature, a technical term for an image of your actual handwritten signature, pasted into your create email signature. How to do this is described below.

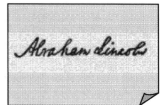

Three ways to create a holographic signature to add to your email:
1. Sign your name on paper and scan it into your computer. Use a dark pen, such as an extra fine "Sharpie." Save this image to your desktop from where you paste it into your signature.
2. Use a digital camera to take a picture of your paper signature and upload the file to your computer, then paste that saved image into your signature.
3. Fax your signature to a service and for about $25 they will reply with a computer file which is a True Type font that can be pasted into your signature. To locate such a service, Google the words "handwritten signature in Outlook."

To add a Signature to Outlook 2007

Open Outlook and follow these steps:

1. Open the Tools menu and select Options
2. In the Options dialog, click the Tab labeled Mail Format
3. Click the button labeled Signatures
4. Click New
5. Enter a name for the signature such as *Internal*
6. Type your name
7. Apply several font types to make it distinct, or insert your holographic signature using the Picture tool
8. Insert your photo using the Picture tool
9. Type in your tag line
10. Click Ok and the signature is created and ready to use

Outlook 2007 also has default options which allow you to choose which email signature to use in your New emails or Replies and Forwards. If you choose *none* as your default, insert the appropriate signature when the message is ready to be sent. Remember to select one of your created signatures before you click send!

To add a Signature to Outlook Express

Adding a plain text signature is easy in Outlook Express, follow these steps:

1. Open the Tools menu and select Options
2. Click the Signatures tab
3. Click New. Text is the default choice. If you want an HTML signature, you need a special file as described below
4. Type the text of your signature under *Edit Signature*
5. Enter the name of your signature file
6. Click Set as Default if you want to have it inserted into every email you send
7. Click OK

Add your business card (VCF) to your Outlook and Outlook Express emails to make it easy for a recipient to add your information to her Outlook contacts.

1. Open the Tools menu and select Options
2. Click the Compose tab
3. At the bottom of this dialog check Mail
4. Pull down the list to locate your name

If you have not created a record with your own information, exit from this dialog and add yourself as a contact in your Outlook address book.

5. Click Edit to make sure the information in your contact record is correct and complete.
6. Click OK.

It is possible to create signatures in HTML for Outlook Express (with pictures and various fonts. To do so requires that you create the file outside of Express and then add it as described above. Instead of the Text option you select File and locate the HTML file you created. The process to create one is outside the scope of my expertise, but the steps to do so are on the web via Google.

Voice Mail Identity

Call your phone number at work and listen to your outgoing personal voice mail message. Do you sound friendly, enthusiastic and professional?

Most outgoing messages are straightforward and predictable.

Ring…ring…ring…

> "You have reached Jenny La Farge at extension 555, please leave a message."

While concise and accurate, this message does not create a memorable impression.

Make your outgoing message memorable and project a professional, image.

First, follow these steps when recording it:
- Stand up
- Take a deep breath
- Look in a mirror
- Smile and record your greeting.

But before you record your message, write it out and rehearse it so you sound genuine and do not falter.

Include a Marketing Me message, such as:

> "Hi, thanks for calling, this is Jenny La Farge, **your problem solving specialist**! Please leave a message…I return all my calls by 4 PM."

OR

> "Hi, this is Douglas Wolf, **your Job Doctor**…please leave a message or if you prefer, send an email to Douglas@MarketingMeBook.com. That's Douglas@MarketingMeBook.com."

Another option is to include your email tagline in your outgoing message.

When you leave a Message

When you *leave* a message, express that same enthusiasm and friendliness. Include your tag line to make sure your message stands out.

A few additional important recommendations about leaving voice mail messages:

- Always repeat your name and number, even if you think the person knows them. We pick up voicemail messages everywhere in the world and sometimes do not have phone numbers handy to call back.
- *Clearly* state your name and say it twice. Cell phones cut in and out and can create havoc with messages. Give the receiver a higher likelihood of hearing your full name.
- When you state your name, remember to say it as *two* words: Avoid running your first and last name together into one word. A slight pause between the two names makes it more clear for someone who may be hearing your name for the first time.

Business Cards

If you have control over the format and contents of your business cards, include the following:

- Your photo
- Your Job Title
- Your Marketing Me Tag Line
- Your Direct phone number

Other Simple ways to be Memorable

Send thank you notes

Keep a box of real paper Thank You notes at your desk. Freely send them to people who help you. Sending Thank You notes is especially useful when what you are thanking the person for may seem to have been part of their routine job. By pointing out how their work is valuable to you, you create a more compelling memory of your interaction with them. They will remember you in a positive way because you remembered to thank them.

Kerry needed a favor from someone in human resources and called Allison, a person she had contacted two years ago. At the beginning of the conversation, Kerry introduced herself, saying, "I don't know if you remember me, but two years ago, you and I worked on this issue." Allison said, "Yes, I remember you. You sent me a thank you note. I'll be happy to help you now." Allison remembered a thank you note she had received two years earlier, making it easier for Kerry to get the help she needed today.

In the Thank You note, specifically mention what the person did for you and how it helped you. Generic phrases, such as, "Thanks for all you do" or "I really appreciated your help last week" are too easy to write and can easily be dismissed. However, a specific thank you like the examples below will probably be taped to the wall in front of that person at their desk.

"Thanks for getting me the answer to that revenue puzzle on Tuesday, the same day I asked for it. Your information made completing my report on time much easier and helped our boss make a good decision about how to solve the problem"

"Jan, your story about our diligence on the Global project in the meeting last week made such a difference in my discussion with the budget team the next day. They all heard how you and I worked over the

Your coworkers can use your thank you notes as we have told you to: to demonstrate the value of their work to their bosses.

weekend to get them accurate and timely numbers and consequently, pushed our requests to the top of the list. I think we'll get more than what we need! Thanks for your support."

The more of these notes you do, the easier it gets to write them. Eventually, you will be known for your generosity.

Distribute Valuable Information

In most companies, using the intranet to send junk email is certainly frowned upon if not grounds for disciplinary action. There are better ways to keep in touch with your colleagues. Your goal is to be helpful and visible.

- Send articles and links to colleagues that they would find valuable
- Be thoughtful with what you forward and to whom so that you do not crowd others' inboxes or be perceived as a nuisance

Other Ways to Increase Your Visibility

Toastmasters

Rather than hunkering down in an economic crisis, my advice is to do the opposite. Heighten your visibility in the Marketing Me ways as I have been describing. Admittedly, it takes confidence to step forward more than you normally do and one resource you can use to build your confidence is Toastmasters International.

> *Mia Ross was a competent school administrator who wanted to improve her chances of promotion in the school district. She joined Toastmasters to hone her presentation skills, an important part of the position she sought. Naturally quiet-spoken and unassuming, after 6 months, she had developed her skills in speaking assertively and declaratorily so much so that she decided to run for office in her school district, thereby increasing her influence exponentially. She decisively defeated her opponent in the following election.*

Toastmasters is the resource for people who fear speaking in front of groups - which is true for over 90% of us. Toastmasters has chapters nearly everywhere which meet on a regular basis. At the meetings, members work together honing presentation skills. You get to practice whatever you want to get better at and get immediate feedback, the preponderance of which is positive and encouraging. It is a low cost way (the organization is non-profit) for you to develop public speaking confidence which in turn will make you more confident about implementing the techniques I describe in Marketing Me.

You can join a local club or get help from Toastmasters to start one at your company – another good way to demonstrate initiative, leadership and gusto. More information about finding or starting a club is at http://www.toastmasters.org.

Service Clubs

Rotary, Lions Clubs, Optimists, Kiwanis, Chamber of Commerce and many other organizations all provide opportunities to build your leadership, teamwork and speaking skills. Participate in a service club that your boss is in or find one that fits your interests and let people know you are active. Activism may pigeonhole you for some people, but those who are active supporters and participants themselves recognize the dedication and effort needed to be a member of any philanthropic or self-improvement group. You have instant rapport with fellow members, a commonality with other activists, and learn job skills as a benefit.

Social Networking

Social networking opportunities abound and new forms seemingly emerge overnight. The original purpose of Facebook or MySpace for was much more socially oriented and most business professionals shied away from their controversial aspect. LinkedIn claims to be focused on building networks of business-only relationships. Check out all three to see which, if any, are more in tune with your organization's culture and audience. Be wary of what you post as the information is completely public.

You gotta have friends...

Once you take the plunge, post your skill set and actively connect to those in your company and in your industry. Devote regular time each week to update and hone your information to ensure you are being sought out by those you truly want to link up with. Position yourself as an expert in your subject area, building your value with those in your company that are linked to you as well as the larger world community. Respond immediately to requests you receive, otherwise people just move on to the next person to get their information. Take advantage of all the features of each site to get the best exposure.

By the time you read this, Facebook should have released an updated version of their software which allows you to clearly separate your personal page from your career or business page. By doing this, you should be able to interact with people in both spheres without having to join several different sites such as LinkedIn, which is mostly used for business networking.

> *One of my clients said: "I've used LinkedIn as my primary social networking site because it tends to focus more on professional connections. For instance, recommendation requests are structured to focus on how you and the person you are recommending worked together. I use it to find colleagues with whom I can collaborate on projects. I have deliberately limited the information I post to prevent unwanted requests to connect. An important feature is their groups. You can join or create your own. They allow for specific topic discussions and exchanges of ideas which\helps create buzz as you participate in them."*

Get your own social network started. For information on how to do that, visit www.howtosoftware.com to view short video lessons on creating your Facebook page.

Twitter

The value of Twitter beyond the voyeur and curiosity aspects is, as this book goes to press, being debated. The CEO of Zappos.com touts its value for being in regular contact with the people that work for Zappos. He sends inspirational, humorous and informational messages regularly and says the interactions and feedback have proved very valuable to keeping Zappos competitive and worker-friendly.

Since the intention of social networking is to build a community of connections, the key to being effective in that endeavor is posting consistent updates. Neglected personal pages, infrequent blogs or rare twitters will cause your followers/connections to lose interest and your community will whither away.

Summary

In this chapter I examined the many different but coordinated ways that you can start to market yourself within your company. From voice mail, email and personal interactions, you can develop a marketing message that elevates you.

Next Chapter

In chapter 7, I cover the techniques to promote yourself in a larger way, when you are ready.

ACTION

☐ Create, rehearse and begin using your Personal Marketing Message.

☐ Spice up your Email signature: become known for your skills and talent.

☐ Update and enhance the outgoing message on your voicemail.

☐ Demonstrate your energy and enthusiasm when you leave messages.

☐ Build your social network and use it to promote your skills and talents.

Marketing Me

Chapter Seven

Step 5: Campaign for Yourself with Big Marketing Me Tactics

In this chapter, I give you ideas for how to launch a more public campaign advancing you above your peers. Your Go Big Marketing Me campaign will make your boss and his boss take notice.

In Chapter 6 I provided you tools to get known within your immediate sphere of influence. If you implemented my suggestions then several outcomes resulted:

- You and your boss started having regular meaningful conversations
- Those interactions engendered a trusting relationship.
- Your work tasks are clear to both you and your boss. This includes future tasks you are willing to take on.
- You have a personal marketing message.
- You can deliver your personal marketing message in a clear, concise and confident manner.
- Your message triggers the receiver to ask you "How do you do that?"
- Your email and voice mail reflect your problem-solving abilities and make you recognizable.
- Your co-workers understand your role in the organization. You are the go-to person for a particular skill or knowledge set

Sandy works for a large corporation with multiple geographic locations. Most of his communication is via email and phone. On a quarterly basis he travels to other sites. He added his picture and tag line to his email signature and was pleasantly surprised at the response. Many of the people he regularly contacted via email and phone instantly recognized him when he arrived at remote sites because of his picture and a few jokingly used his tagline as a way of saying hello.

If you have undertaken all the actions I described in prior chapters, without immediate success, be patient. Your Marketing Me campaign takes time to have an effect. It may take your boss or colleagues three months or more before they start giving you positive feedback.

Your Big Marketing Me Campaign

The tactics you can employ in your Marketing Me campaign are dependent upon your job level and skill set. I suggest several in this chapter.

Company Publications

Many companies have internal publications to which you can contribute. They might be in electronic or paper form. Your name on a submission lifts your profile within the company.

So, what do you write about? Here are a host of topics that are interesting to company readers:

- Increase in sales for the year, month or quarter
- New product or service introduction
- Retirement of a product or service
- New hires
- Stories about long-time employees
- Retirement of an employee
- Seminars attended by sales teams, marketing teams, or design teams
- New machine that increases productivity
- Changes in laws that affect the product or service you support
- Birthdays in your department this month

The list is limited only by your imagination. Some large companies even have a full time staff for in-house publications offering different newsletters for various divisions of the company. One thing you can bet on: They are all dying for content!

You write?!
We love you!

Share your idea for an article with the editor and see if you can get submission credit. You may only need to suggest an idea to get credit. Someone on the publication staff will write it up.

If you write the submission, follow these guidelines:
- Put yourself in the mind of the reader. What will he find interesting? Why?
- Keep your story short and to the point.
- Make sure names are spelled correctly and all details are correct. Nothing ruins your credibility faster than bad information.
- Have someone edit the submission. Every writer needs an editor!

Journalists have a formula for writing news stories and it is to answer these questions: *Who, What, When, Where, Why, and How.*

Your task is to determine the most important aspect of the story and answer that question first. If is a story about a person, the *Who* aspect is your lead sentence. If it is about a seminar people attended, it is the *What* question. Answer any of the six questions to start your story. Once you have submitted a well written, interesting story, you can count on being asked for more contributions.

Ideas for submissions to Company Newsletters or Blogs

You may be the internal expert on a topic or have solved a problem that many people in your company encounter, such as how to customize a report from the data base. Publish an article that tells how to solve that problem. This accomplishes two objectives: you become known as the go-to person for this problem, and you help others become more efficient.

Naomi works for a large corporation in the IT department. As part of her job, she generates report documents that are crucial to hundreds of project managers for accounting purposes. The project managers rely on her for the reports and call her for help interpreting the data in the reports. She determined that most of them called her with a half dozen of the same questions and decided that her time would be better spent documenting the answers to that set of questions processes and publishing them in the division newsletter. To get approval from her boss to submit them to the newsletter, her strategy was to make sure he understood how it would benefit him: her time would be freed up from answering the same few questions over and over. Her boss Ok'd her suggestion. She contacted the newsletter and they agreed to publish her series of answers and tips on how to better use the reporting tool she supported. The results were great! She received many emails from project managers thanking her for documenting their oft-asked questions and said they were happy to know she was the go-to person for help, and since her picture was included more people recognized her. More questions were submitted that she could answer in the future. Her boss was very happy because she now had more time for other projects.

Writing for Industry Publications

One of the fastest ways to get known is to write for industry or professional publications. For instance, you are in the finance department and want to become known as an expert on a specific type of investment. Investigate the most read media for readers interested in that information. Review the industry or professional publications you read, find out what other finance experts read, and choose publications that have the readers who would value your expertise.

Once you identify the correct publication(s), contact the editor with a query via email or letter. (Query is the proper name for a question or request to a media editor.) Editors prefer written queries because they want to know if you can write well in a letter or email. Consider it a sample of your writing. An editor will ignore you if you are unable to posit a coherent, concise query.

Your query letter or email should include the following:
- Your complete contact information
- Your *Curriculum Vitae* - Latin meaning "the course of one's life or career." In other words, list your education and expert credentials.
- Do not worry if you do not have a PhD in your subject area. It is more important that you can prove that you have practical working knowledge of the subject matter.
- Outline of your article and a 2-3 sentence summary
- Copies of prior published articles or a one-two page written sample of your publication subject
- Length in words of your proposed submission
- Date you can deliver the final submission

Expect a 90-day delay from submission to publication. Plan ahead and make sure your topic will not be out of date for the time of year for which you wish to submit it.

> Tip: *Never miss a publishing or submission deadline. Editors have very strict timelines and if you neglect them, you will never write for that publication again and the word gets around to the other editors.*

After submitting the query letter, give the editor a few days to review your query and respond. If the editor liked your idea, he or she will take your call or contact you immediately. If the editor rejects your idea then ask what you could do to improve or reposition the article or topic to make it more likely the editor would publish it with a resubmission

Ideas for submissions to Company Newsletters or Blogs

You may be the internal expert on a topic or have solved a problem that many people in your company encounter, such as how to customize a report from the data base. Publish an article that tells how to solve that problem. This accomplishes two objectives: you become known as the go-to person for this problem, and you help others become more efficient.

Vendor Relationships

You may be important – or the sole - point of contact for a vendor to your company. The vendor is interested in how you use their product and its positive results. Leverage the vendor-sales relationship.

- Write a case study on how you use their service to turn a higher profit.
- Recommend the rep share the study with their other clients and potential customers.
- Offer to speak to people thinking of purchasing the product you use on behalf of the vendor. Get your boss' approval for this action
- Ask for reprints of the case study (or for the link to the posting on the Vendor's website) to add to your Performance Review.

Write a Book

It used to be nearly impossible to write a book and get it published. You had to not only write the book but purchase several hundred copies and promote your book yourself. Even today, very few books are published by the big publishing houses and fewer become best sellers.

However, there is another option. You can self-publish. It is a matter of organizing your material and contacting any of the print-on-demand publishers. Most of these services will get you an International Standard Book Number or ISBN. An ISBN registers your book with the Library of Congress and Amazon so people can easily find your book by subject keywords.

More importantly, you add a published book to your resume. Keep a copy on your desk to market yourself at work. Add "Author of *name of your book*" as a tagline to your email signature and business card.

Speaking

I touched on speaking in the prior chapter and recommended Toastmasters as a positive environment to gain comfort speaking to groups. When you become an experienced speaker, offer to speak at company events or industry conferences. Anything more than two speeches is an experienced speaker.

Contact your company's public relations office and market yourself as an expert speaker. Note you are willing to speak to community groups or at other events where a speaker is requested with your expertise.

Public relations offices require a biography, photo, curriculum vita and any published articles, books or awards. Use your tag line to help them market your expertise and put you in front of audiences. Eventually, the public relations office will request your speech outline and availability.

> Tip: *Do not create your presentation in PowerPoint. Use the outline view in Word then find clip art or jpgs to illustrate your points on slides. Slide after slide of text is literally mind numbing.*

Next thing you know - you will be on Oprah!

Presenting

A few quick tips about presentations:
- Do not read from your slides during your presentation.
- Do not use slides that are only text.
- Be known for engaging your audience.
- Provide your audience with valuable information in your verbal presentation, not reading information off your slides, which the audience could read on their own time.

Summary

With your micro-Marketing Me campaign in operation, the next step, described in this chapter, is to expand your campaign to public forums. Use the many forums available to you; your company newsletter, speaking to community groups or writing for trade publications.

Next Chapter

In Chapter 8, I explain the importance of ensuring your activities are aligned with your company's goals. I show you how to make certain your contributions are on target and valued by your colleagues and boss.

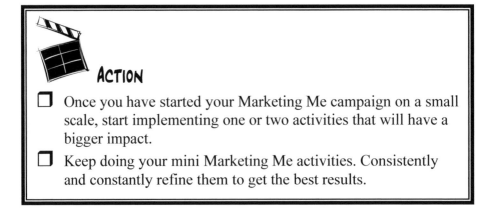

ACTION

☐ Once you have started your Marketing Me campaign on a small scale, start implementing one or two activities that will have a bigger impact.

☐ Keep doing your mini Marketing Me activities. Consistently and constantly refine them to get the best results.

Chapter Eight

Step 6: Align Your Skills with Your Company Needs

In this chapter, I explain how to align the presentation of your skills with the needs of your boss and the company. You also learn how to anticipate and prepare for future challenges.

Recognize Business Cycles

Understanding business cycles is another tool in your Marketing Me plan. Cycles of change are constant factors in business. Old markets fade. New markets emerge. Technology changes the way products are manufactured. Culture determines which products are winners and losers. For example, yesterday the hot product everyone owned was the transistor radio. Today it is the IPod. This is the nature of business cycles.

Your company had specific needs they expected you to address when you were hired for your present job. But as circumstances change, the reason you were originally hired may no longer exist or may be about to undergo substantial change because of business cycles. These changes are predictable more often than not. Many occur in cycles. It is important that you proactively transform your contributions to take advantage of the changes.

For example, when the economic outlook was more positive, people spent money freely on items they *wanted* beyond their basic needs. Examples of this free spending are luxury good such as jewelry, high-end clothing, larger cars, and luxury services such as car detailing. Luxury goods and services are particularly vulnerable to declining economies. Therefore, as the economy shrank, extravagant spending slowed.

Oh a Salad Squirter!!

If you are hired by a company that provides luxury services during an economic upswing, you are vulnerable to being laid off during a downswing. To keep your job, you must reposition your skills or repurpose your position to align with the new business needs of your company.

You may have experienced business cycles in your current or previous job. Think back to how you succeeded during those changes:

- How did you help your boss or co-workers with the changes?
- Did you learn new technology or software applications?
- Were you able to train others on new ways of doing their jobs?
- Did you maintain a positive attitude that helped your coworkers focus on the important tasks instead of complaining about change?

Talk to your boss about your positive past experience during business changes and let him know you are ready to help out in anyway to make the transition smooth as your business moves through a cycle.

Start increasing your awareness of how business cycles play out in your company's plans. As part of your Marketing Me plan, diligently study these cycles to anticipate how you will contribute and add value during different stages of the cycles. The sections that follow offer my recommendations for doing this during different business cycles.

> *Thrift, even among the rich, is the new ethic.*
> *N.Y. Times February 09*

Recognize Product Life Cycles

Does your job directly rely upon one specific product your company provides? If so, be mindful of where the product fits in the product lifecycle. This knowledge assists you in aligning your skills with the product cycle. You can also apply this information to anticipate how you will contribute as the product moves to the next stage.

Below are the standard stages and attributes of a product life cycle:

1. Market Introduction stage
   - costs are high
   - sales volumes are low
   - little or no competition - competitive manufacturers are watching for acceptance or the new product
   - demand is created
   - customers are prompted to try the product

2. Growth stage
   - costs are reduced due to economies of scale
   - sales volume increases significantly
   - profitability begins to rise
   - customer awareness increases
   - competition begins to increase leading to price decreases

3. Mature stage
   - costs lower as production volumes increases
   - sales volume peaks and market saturation is reached
   - more competitors enter the market; prices drop
   - to maintain or increase market share brand differentiation and feature diversification are emphasized
   - profits and margin decline

4. Saturation and Decline stage
   - costs continue to increase
   - sales volume declines or stabilizes
   - prices, profitability diminish
   - production/distribution efficiency affects profits more than sales

Take a moment and determine which stage your product is in. If the job you perform relates to a product entering into a new stage, proactively determine what actions you can take that will be valuable.

> *Deadlines are the mothers of invention.*
> *John M. Shanahan,*
> *Inventor*

For example, if your product is moving from the Market Introduction stage to Growth, anticipate that your company must meet higher production schedules to maximize profits through economies of scale. Look into opportunities to assist in meeting that challenge and convey ideas to your boss.

If the product is in the Saturation and Decline stage, consider finding another product to support – perhaps even asking for a transfer. As a product enters this final stage, management usually retires or sells it to another firm. In either case, your job may no longer be needed. Be ready to reposition your skills and knowledge to new or different products.

The Hummer® exemplifies a product in the Saturation and Decline stage. It was a popular display of extravagance and Hummer sales were respectable. In the summer of 2008, high gas prices deterred new buyers, moving the Hummer from the Mature to the Decline stage. In response, GM tried to extend the Hummer's longevity by decreasing its size and repositioning it as a "new" product. However, the cost and maintenance of a large vehicle like the Hummer in a declining economy will likely end its production and the jobs it provided.

Service Life Span

Many services undergo changes that are not cyclical but rather have a definite life span. The means of providing the services change. Some services become obsolete while others evolve.

Some constantly evolving service professions and roles are:
- Accounting (tax rules change)
- Medical billing (insurance billing codes change)
- Paralegal (updates to relevant laws occur monthly)
- Healthcare (new medicines and delivery systems are made available regularly)

Version
10.2.5.3.70a

If you are in a service profession that constantly evolves, learn what is new and relevant to your profession in anticipation of their implementation at your company. Your job is secure as long as you keep up with changes.

Take classes about changes in, for instance, accounting rules and relevant government regulations. Then, tell your boss that you have completed these self-improvement activities. Suggest ways you can help your department and company with your new knowledge or skill.

If your company is in a declining service business, ask yourself:
- What research are you doing to determine how you will reposition *your* knowledge or skills?
- Have your found ways to integrate new technologies into your work or service process?

> Even President Obama has a garden!

- How is your company positioning itself to lure or keep consumers who are leading a culture changes, such as the demand for greener packaging?
- What ways can your company increase customer convenience?

These questions and suggestions stimulate the Marketing Me process: be proactive and innovative to position yourself as valuable beyond your excellent work skills.

Disruptions and Dynamic Changes

A disruption is a dramatic change in the way an industry or profession does business. For instance, the proliferation of personal computers and the internet disrupted the travel industry. Travel agencies provided airline tickets, car rentals and travel packages for business or personal travel. Today, travel agencies are dwindling since people and companies now book travel reservations via the internet.

Eighty-eight percent of consumers who...plan to travel...use the web to research and purchase their trips.

The nearly-extinct travel agency industry was not subject to a life cycle or a services span. It was the casualty of a disruption. Technological innovation made travel agency services obsolete.

Dynamic change is an internal technology

cycle: It is the process of supplanting the old way of doing things by new technology. Dynamic change affects every industry.

Prepare to change *before* a disruption or dynamic change takes over your profession or industry. Update your knowledge or upgrade your skills before you boss or the company tells you to.

For example, become the first expert to use new software. Many software features go unused because people do not take the time to completely learn them. Become proficient at using your company's software tools and capabilities. Tell others that you know the software extremely well.

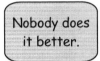

Nobody does it better.

You become essential by being able to correct others' errors, or prevent them from making errors. Be the subject matter expert and trainer on that software. These are valuable contributions.

Perhaps you have a talent for design. You quickly learn MS Publisher to assist laying out the company newsletter. But, you need help with the mail merge function to distribute the newsletter. Partner up with someone who is skilled at mail merge. You contribute a valuable skill and become part of the organizational communication team. You have also taught yourself a valuable skill that you can use in any position.

The Marketing Me lessons:

1. If your job becomes replaceable by new technologies, business cycles or service life spans, prepare to find a new role or retrain yourself for your imminent future at your present job
2. Learn new technology early, before anyone else learns it.
3. When you learn something new, tell your boss how it will benefit *him* and the company.
4. Seek out ways to put your new knowledge or skill to good use for your company

Seasonal Cycles

Many companies are in industries whose products or services follow the seasons of the year. Most retail stores plan to make most of their annual profit from sales in the 4th quarter. Food producing companies in the Midwest are locked into the calendar of spring planting, summer crop tending and fall harvesting.

Consider anticipating the seasonal cycle in your business, and offer ideas to improve production or services prior to their need arising.

Many companies have recurring problems that occur during one season. Solving a seasonal problem is often

> Whew! That's done until next year!

neglected because the problem occurs only once per year. If you recognize a recurring problem, determine a solution. Take the initiative to present your idea to your boss. Do not leave fixing recurring problems to someone else.

Ask yourself:

- Do the same problems, such as lost materials, crop up every year during your annual inventory?
- Do you rush around to package and send out trade show supplies the night before set-up?
- Is your purchasing department consistently late submitting its product order for quarterly promotional events?
- Is there a mad rush at your company to stock shelves in December?

> *A warehouse company completed inventory every January. Traditionally, everyone in the company was expected to participate in order to get the enormous task done in one day. Unfortunately, inexperienced non-warehouse employees made significant counting mistakes that regular warehouse personnel had to remedy, took late into the night and incurred significant overtime. After one inventory, a warehouse employee suggested using temps to do the counting and bringing them in one day early to train them and therefore reduce errors. The warehouse manager implemented the idea the following year. The cost of using temps, even for an extra day, incurred no overtime, costing far less. The employee was given a bonus for the idea. Within six months, he was promoted to Assistant Warehouse Manager.*

Cultural Cycles

Styles change and societal rules and norms are malleable. Products become obsolete overnight or vault to be best sellers. If your product or service fits the current culture, it likely will stay profitable. However, if suddenly it is *not* a fit, you can be looking for work very quickly.

The Chia pet and Cabbage Patch Dolls are examples of products that quickly rose and fell in popularity. Another prominent example occurred in 1960 when John F. Kennedy was elected to the presidency. He did not wear a top hat to his inauguration, a tradition of at least 150 years. Suddenly, no man in America wanted to look out of date and sales of all hats fell to nearly nothing. One gesture effectively destroyed an entire industry as the cultural cycle changed.

The development of electronic media has completely changed the recording industry. Freely sharing music is now the cultural norm.

What else changed as a result? Copyright and intellectual property protection technology has evolved. Music sharing websites have proliferated and CD sales are nearly nonexistent. Music stores that sold CDs are closing. Technology changes drove this dynamic change. But sharing music via the internet, cell phones and playlists on websites solidified the culture change.

Plastic drinking water bottles have succumbed to the culture change that emphasizes "green" packaging. Companies that produce reusable stainless steel water bottles have capitalized on this wave and are profiting.

What changes are on the horizon for your industry? Read trade journals and forward-looking publications and websites. One of my favorites is Seth Godin's blog where he has an innovative way to look at marketing. Godin is the author of Meatball Sundae and other leading edge marketing books.

What's the Purple Cow at our company?

Stay on top of the major changes in how our society uses products and services and you will anticipate culture changes. When you recognize a new trend that is relevant to your company or your job, research how others are taking advantage of the coming change. Present those and your own ideas to your boss.

Summary

Keeping your job in tough times requires that you market yourself to your boss and to your company with a consistent message. But you must be aware of the revenue stream that supports your job and how it can change. Being in alignment with the strategies of your company as it adjusts to business cycles gives you the ability to be proactive and implement Marketing Me actions.

Guidelines for aligning your skills:
- Assess your work and ask questions about the products and services your firm offers.
- Get a firm grasp of the internal and external cycles that affect your products.

- Anticipate and learn the new technologies that will make your work more valuable than your co-workers'.
- Let the boss know when you believe you have a solution to a recurring problem.

Make yourself a job-keeper not a job-seeker!

Next Chapter

In chapter 9, I provide guidance on the tools to best organize and track your Marketing Me campaign.

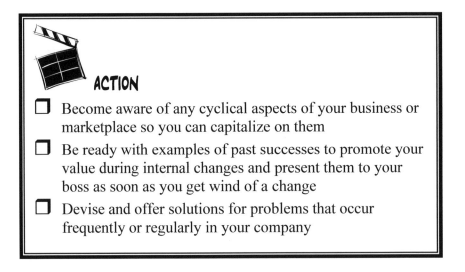

ACTION

☐ Become aware of any cyclical aspects of your business or marketplace so you can capitalize on them

☐ Be ready with examples of past successes to promote your value during internal changes and present them to your boss as soon as you get wind of a change

☐ Devise and offer solutions for problems that occur frequently or regularly in your company

Chapter Nine

Step 7: Organize Your Marketing Me Campaign

In this chapter, I describe how to best organize your tasks to implement your Marketing Me campaign.

I have been recommending actions in each chapter that I know are valuable and get results. But the likelihood you have actually done all of them – or even a good portion of them - is low. This is not because you are not excited or enthusiastic, but I gave you a *lot* to do. This chapter is your call to action and helps you organize and prioritize your action steps.

Marketing Me is a strategic campaign with the objective of keeping your job. With that clear objective in mind, your tactics should be organized around a plan and a calendar.

You have only so much time...

Perhaps you have experienced this unbending rule: there are only so
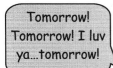
many hours in a day and so many days in a week into which you can fit your activities, both personal and professional. The rule is based upon the fact that there are only 168 hours in a week: how are you going to allocate them?

Most people do not think of the number of hours in a week as finite. There is a tendency to believe "I'll find the time" or "I'll work on it tomorrow". There is no way to *find* time: You have 168 hours and that is it!

Assume that 168 hours per week IS a deadline and roughly 50 hours are what most people have to get work activities completed!

Carefully and purposefully consider how you use those precious hours. Then plan your activities, plotting each one in a calendar as appointments with yourself to complete your Marketing Me work.

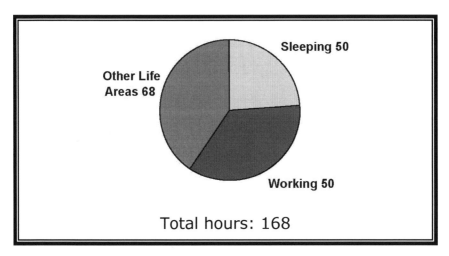

Total hours: 168

Assess your Progress

After reading the previous chapters, you must have implemented a few of the ideas. Before you add more, take time to assess the effectiveness of those actions. This is not an exhaustive, scientific evaluation, just a pause to reflect and think back on how things are going.

Start with these questions:

- If you have taken advantage of opportunities to speak up at meetings about your completed and successful action items or projects, what kind of responses did you get?
  - Did people follow up to ask you additional questions?
  - Did your boss let on that he had heard you have been talking up your achievements?
  - Did you get more assignments or responsibility as a result?

- Consider how you have changed the way you provide your boss with information: are you continuing to base this upon your evaluation of his communication style?
  - Is he listening more closely to you or responding to your emails more readily?
  - Does he approach you more often to consult on concerns or projects?
  - Is he more disposed to linger and chat with you after meetings?

- What about changes you have made to your presentation of your work and value to the company? What has been the response?
  - o Have you updated your email signature?
  - o Have you tested different tag lines and asked for feedback?
  - o Are you being asked *how* you do what you do?

- If you have taken classes or asked for training on a specific topic, have you told your boss what you have learned?

  > What did you learn in school today?

  - o As a result, have you been approached about new responsibilities? Or been given a raise?

- How are your efforts to connect with people who can influence the decision of whether you stay or go?
  - o Have you checked some names off that list as "on your side"?
  - o Have you been able to get in front of higher-ups with ideas or contributions?

- What else have you done?
- What are your results so far?
  - o Which of your results can you monetize (tie directly to increased revenue or savings for your company or you)
  - o How much are your result worth in total so far?
  - o What has given you the best results? What makes you think that? Are those results measurable? Have they increased recognition of your value?

After taking stock of how your efforts are proceeding and the results you are getting, you will find you are eager to do more. Hone what you have started and evolve into a true Marketing Me campaigner.

> *Progress comes from the intelligent use of experience.*
> *Elbert Hubbard, Philosopher*

Next steps

Refer to the Activity Tracking spreadsheet (available on my website in the Resources section) and begin prioritizing the next set of 2-3 activities you are going to undertake. Plan these activities so that you are not cramming them in or that your previously implemented activities get neglected. Be deliberate with what action you choose to do. Use your previous results to help direct your new efforts.

What if I am not getting the results I want?

A number of things can get in the way of your initiatives, as in any marketing campaign. I will examine a few of the obvious hurdles first, because they are readily identifiable and easily correctible.

1. I have a hard time getting a regular meeting with my boss. If you are not meeting with your boss at least once a month, your first step is to request and set up ad hoc or informal meetings. These need to last only about 15 minutes. If you and he meet monthly, then ask for a brief 10-15 minute "betweener" about 10 working days after each regular meeting. Your aim is to meet at a more frequent interval than your regularly scheduled meetings.

It is *very* important that you stick to that short meeting length of 15 minutes, demonstrating that you respect your boss' time.
- Have your agenda ready, perhaps emailing it to him prior to your meeting, and stick to it.
- At the end of the 15 minutes, offer to end the meeting. Perhaps say, "I'm sure you've got other things going on. Thanks for this meeting and I'll follow up with you later."
- Establish this impression of respect and the pattern of brief meetings and it is likely he will be more amenable to having them with you.

> **Tip:** *After any meeting with your boss in which you got action items, send him an email noting the tasks and due dates. This assures you're in agreement about what needs to be done AND adds to your record of accomplishments.*

Now the prospect is likely that you will stay top of mind and be able to cover more topics in days or weeks instead of having to wait for another month to pass before you get in his office again.

Remember, accommodate how you connect to his preferred communication style: Phone or email may be better for him. Perhaps it would be easier to set up a specific, brief time on a regular basis when you talk on the phone. You boss may have a long commute or shuttling frequently from meeting to meeting. While phone time is not necessarily as productive, it may be more practical. I also recommend that you continue your efforts to request face to face meeting from time to time.

2. I'm not involved in many project meetings or any meetings except with my boss

This is a sign that you have not positioned yourself to be noticed for your achievements and contributions. It is time you start asking around about how to get involved in committees, projects, teams, boards. Initially, you may have to consent to help with an office party or charity event or another non-work related activity.

Be sure to do your best work, while not letting these low-priority activities interfere with your highest priorities of doing A+++ work and your other Marketing Me activities.

Second, choose wisely and do not work on projects that will not be noticed by your boss or other decision makers. Do not volunteer to do activities that are risky or for which you have no skill. Focus on what you know, contributing your expertise and knowledge, making your mark every step of the way. Most importantly, be sure your activities are forwarding your goal of promoting yourself and your capabilities.

3. I can not find time to do many of the things suggested.

If you knew your job was in jeopardy, that your lay-off date was next month, would you believe you did not have time? In this economy, you have a deadline. The reality is that your job is not guaranteed. You must find time and make the effort to market yourself.

> *Steve was a highly competent and effective long-term contract worker for a major software company. Upon hearing the concept of this book, he shot back, with dismay in his voice, "Geez. I'm not doing any of those things and my job is at a pretty high risk because I'm a contractor: It's easy to get me off the payroll." He immediately initiated some of the activities we recommend and discovered several opportunities that could extend his contract.*

Now it is time to discuss your calendar as it relates to the time hurdle.

Your Activity Calendar

This calendar is a record of your Marketing Me tactics and results as well as a scheduling tool. If you do not have a desktop calendar or a PDA or other means to schedule and record your activities, get one. It can be paper or electronic as long as you are comfortable with it and will use it everyday.

> *To choose time is to save time.*
> Francis Bacon

Your calendar organizes your activities, builds your never-ending performance review, and gives you a snapshot of your progress.

The one thing you will immediately notice is how many opportunities you actually have to be proactive and promote yourself. You want to capitalize on every one.

Just to get started and be proactively organized, get accustomed to using your calendar rather than a To Do list as your organizing tool. Start making appointments with yourself for all your activities as a way of ensuring you actually do them and that you accurately track what you complete.

Here are the major calendar activities you must do:

Coming up! Don't touch that remote!

1. Review upcoming events. Determine what opportunities exist for you to market yourself. Schedule time to prepare, whether it is gathering information and documents, reviewing the agenda, or just thinking about how you will take advantage of this opportunity.

2. From now on, after every meeting you attend, make extensive notes. You can do this on your calendar or your tracking sheet – or both.
   a. Record the attendees (especially if they are decision makers/your boss)
   b. Note the topic
   c. Describe how you promoted your achievements and value
   d. Note how you contributed knowledge or expertise

3. At the end of each week, look ahead to the next week and determine if you have at least one activity per day to market yourself. Add tasks so you have at least one per working day.
   a. Choose the most productive activities from your review of your previous tactics
   b. Add new types of activities one at a time, repeating them if necessary to fill your calendar.

Marketing Me Calendar example

You scheduled meetings on Monday, Wednesday and Friday Plan how you will contribute. For Tuesday and Thursday, schedule time to write articles which is a new Marketing Me activity. Here is what your Marketing Me activities might look like on your calendar:

©2009 by Douglas J. Wolf

Your notes on those activities:

- **Monday**: Meeting on Project budget – mention coming under projections for paper <u>costs</u>
- **Tuesday**: Schedule 10 minutes to write <u>article</u> for company NL on "Going Green"
- **Wednesday**: Team Meeting with Boss: Tell him we have the <u>revisions</u> done ahead of schedule because I taught the team how to use on-line document collaboration tool
- **Thursday**: Schedule 30 minutes to write up instructions on document collaboration tool as article for newsletter to share with whole company, Call Teleconference facilitator to get "Going Green" on agenda for Friday's call
- **Friday**: Division Teleconference – Make announcement about "Going Green" initiative and article in newsletter for everyone to read
  a. Be sure you actually schedule time to write the articles and prepare for activities like the Teleconference.

  b. Use your own time if the activities are not directly related to your priority project. Still put the time to write it on your calendar and keep that appointment with yourself.

4. At the beginning of each month, examine what opportunities are looming. Schedule time to prepare for and attend each.

Add activities so you are doing at least one per working day, even if it is as simple as responding to an email. Remember, each message you send has your Marketing Me signature and tag line and counts as promoting you.

Done...done... done...done... done!

As you get better at organizing your activities, you will find you do simple ones automatically. At that point, add more complex or sophisticated tactics.

Continuously upgrade your awareness of how to communicate with your boss. Refine your skill at flexing your style to connect with other decision-makers. Use and hone your powers of observation to improve your skills building those important relationships.

Just the act of looking ahead will benefit your ability to take advantage of opportunities. Continue to refine your strategy and discipline:

- Prepare materials for meetings
- Think about upcoming events and plan how you will contribute
- Contact meeting leaders to get on agendas
- Put time on your schedule for preparation and honor those appointments. They are just as important as the actual meetings.

Wallflowers will not make it in this economy.

Greg Goates, Sr. Director
Leadership Development, Amylin Pharmaceuticals

Time Allocation Accuracy

Have you ever started a project and once into it discovered that it will take you much more time than you thought? Or started doing something and figured out you can get it done very quickly?

A vital result from calendaring and tracking your activities is your discovery of how long it *actually* takes you to complete a task. When you first do some of the Marketing Me activities, track how much time you used to complete the task. Then the next time you do that activity you will know how much time to schedule for it.

Time is on *my* side...

For instance, you choose to allocate 20 minutes to write a quick blog entry for your company site. But actually you used 45 minutes. Next time, you know to schedule at least 45 minutes for this activity.

Remember to keep copies of everything you do and use those to create templates for future work. For instance, if you write emails for co-workers to edit and then forward to your boss as testimonials, keep copies of what you send and file them in a Marketing Me folder for quick access. You will find them easily the next time you ask someone to write you a testimonial.

The more you do to promote yourself, the better and more efficient you will get at doing the activities, and the more likely you will get the results you seek.

> *Every successful man I have heard of has done the best he could with conditions as he found them, and not waited until the next year for better.*
>
> *Edgar Watson Howe, Journalist*

What if I am still not getting results?

As they said in the movie Apollo 13, "Houston, we have a problem." I know the Marketing Me strategies work, but there are exceptions.

Here are a few of them:
- You have previously established a troublesome reputation with your boss, and he is not open to changing his perception. While this is not fatal, it is a big hurdle and merits individual intervention. You need a professional coach to help remedy this relationship. (Check my website Resources section for a Coach who has this expertise.)
- You have alienated a lot of your colleagues who are now unwilling to acknowledge your contributions, expertise or advocate for you. Again, not fatal, but it will take a lot of repair work and may not be worth it
- Your company is sinking fast and

Coaching is a developmental process based on identifying and building on one's strengths, eliminating barriers to success and achieving results.

no one is paying attention to anything but preserving their own job. Get your resume out into the marketplace

- Your communication, social or interaction skills are underdeveloped. You would benefit from a professional coach.
- Other – none of the above seem to fit and you can not figure it out. Again, this situation calls for specific diagnosis and remedy from an expert other than you.

Summary

This chapter gave you many tools and ideas for organizing yourself and your Marketing Me campaign. Those tools and ideas help you maintain a consistent and rewarding effort to keep your job.

You now have all Seven Steps of your Marketing Me Plan to keep your job!

Step 1: *Change your Mindset*

Step 2: *Understand your Marketing Me Target Market: Your Boss*

Step 3: *Build Your Own Performance Review*

Step 4: *Campaign for Yourself: Your Micro Marketing Me activities*

Step 5: *Campaign for Yourself: Big Marketing Me activities*

Step 6: *Align Your Skills with the Needs of your Company*

Step 7: *Organize your Marketing Me Campaign*

Next Chapter

In Chapter 10, we examine the personal obstacles that may stop you from putting what you have learned into action. I show you how to overcome those obstacles.

ACTION

- ☐ Track the Marketing Me activities you have done, who you targeted, and your results.
- ☐ Add a new Marketing Me activity or more intensity to current activities every 30 days
- ☐ Continue the activities that get you the results you seek
- ☐ Engage a professional coach to help you overcome hurdles if you are not getting the results you want. Go to www.MarketingMe.US or MarketingMeBookj.com to find the right coach for your situation.

Chapter Ten: Why you Might Not Do This

In this chapter, we examine the personal obstacles that may stop you from putting all seven steps of your Marketing Me campaign into action. I then show you how to overcome those obstacles.

Most people start these kinds of life-changing projects and do not continue. Some people quit at the *first* hurdle. There are as many reasons **why** people quit as there are people.

Remember learning to ride a bike? At first you could not get any part of it under control. Your feet kept slipping off the pedals, you could not steer straight, and forget about braking! When you are first attempting something new, you feel awkward, reluctant and resistant. Because of this, humans choose to remain the same much more readily than we choose to change…unless there is an emergency – a strong motivator.

The swiftness of time is infinite… Did you ever pull an all-nighter to finish homework? Pull a proposal off the printer minutes before meeting with the client? Gone out for a forgotten ingredient ten minutes before a dinner party? We do *these* things - despite their difficulty - because we are motivated by a deadline.

This is an evolutionary response: Our brains are wired to wait until danger is right in front of us before we take action. Therefore, to make changes, especially difficult or atypical, we need deadlines (interesting term…).

> *Better three hours too soon, than one minute too late.*
> *William Shakespeare*

Excuses, excuses…

We humans are absolutely brilliant at justifying our decisions to stay the same and not do things differently. Additionally, as a bonus, we convince ourselves that we are making the best decision.

Here are excuses which I have heard – and used– and know that you will recognize:
- You do not believe that your talents and skills are actually that important or valuable
- Others will make fun of your efforts to "suck up"
- You think you will be sticking your neck out too far
- You doubt you can carry it off…you will look insincere, "fake" or manipulative
- You do not have time
- You will not be able to keep track of everything
- You will not be able to do these things 100% so you would rather just skip it (the all-or-nothing thinking of perfectionism)
- You will get to it someday when things are "better"
- Someone else is already doing this stuff and you will look like a copy-cat
- You are afraid of what others will think of you:
  - "Who does she think *she* is?"
  - "She's only trying to be treated special…"
  - "He's the boss's favorite."
  - "He's in a special category…"
  - "She only got ahead because she…"

> I'm fine just as I am, thank you.

…and so on.

You have probably invented a few of your own while reading this book. So, to quote my former boss, "Which would you rather have in two years; good excuses or a better life?"

Lose the mindset that you need to be excused from responsibility for your life. You either do or don't do - to paraphrase Master Yoda.

> *Undertake something that is difficult; it will do you good.*
> *Unless you try to do something beyond what you have already*
> *mastered, you will never grow.*
>
> *Ronald E. Osborn, Author and Dean*

What is the worst thing that could happen?

If you decide to go forward and implement these ideas, most likely your esteem will go up in the minds of your co-workers and your boss.

Can not get your mind around that notion? Then discuss all the worst things you think could happen. Say them out loud and examine this other side of this concern: Even though these things *could* happen, what is the likelihood they will? Instead of thinking about the worst things that could happen, focus on the *best* outcomes:

- You could get promoted
- You could be invited into high-visibility projects
- You could really put your talents to use and make a significant contribution to your company.
- You could have fun.
- You might even keep your job.

The world of work is not a level playing field, organizations are not rational. According to David D'Alessandro in <u>Career Warfare</u>, companies are "full of eccentricity, rashness, and pettiness. Like small towns they are driven by gossip, intrigue and anecdote." What is your best response? Take risks - the ones *you* want to take - not those that are driven by the capriciousness of the economy or the peculiar culture of your company.

> No minute lost
> Comes ever back again.
> Take heed and see
> Ye do nothing in vain.
> *Motto on the London*
> *Clock Tower*

Get off the couch

Given that most of us are procrastinators and masters of the couch potato pose, another method to make change, as I initially explained in

Chapter 3, is to act "as if."

In the weight reduction world, once people choose to change their eating habits, the constant mantra of "act as if" is their psychological mindset to support change that initially seems overwhelming and impossible. Think about it -we are all immersed in a culture intricately woven with food and eating. A dieter has to stay away from environments where the food may be too tempting ("all-you-can-eat" buffets.) Furthermore, a dieter must find new social activities that do not always involve food and cope with relationships with family and friends without the social cushion of eating. This is a monumental change in thinking, decision-making and behavior. What works? Among other things, the mantra, "act as if." For a dieter, act as if you are a healthy person, act as if you have control over your food choices, act as if you care about your health.

This mindset provides discipline, direction and support. The "as if" concept reassures these uncertain people who at first feel awkward giving up the hidden stash of comfort food, feel weird socializing without involving a meal. It takes assertiveness to request special foods at a restaurant, and so on. People soon recognized that they have to *act* differently until it feels "normal".

Your Marketing Me campaign is like this – a significant change in behavior that requires a new mindset.

Time is money.

Benjamin Franklin

The Twenty-one Day Rule

Research shows you have to consistently complete a new behavior at least once per day for at least 21 consecutive days (30 is better) for it to become a habit. This is one reason I recommend doing only 2-3 new Marketing Me activities. Build a habit over 30 days with a small set before you add new behaviors. And remember, it has to be *consecutive* days. If you skip a day, you have to start over. Do not be mad at me for that! This is your brain, one stubborn piece of equipment that we are trying to change.

> **To quote from Oprah's magazine O!, in the article, "Why Is It So Damn Hard To Change?" published in January 2007, written by Rebecca Skloot:**
>
> "You're doing nothing less than rewiring your brain. Approach change as if you're learning a new language or a new instrument. Overcoming an unhealthy habit involves changing the behaviors associated with it and managing stress, because stressing about change (or anything else) will knock you off the wagon faster than you realize. Above all, get that dopamine system going: Find rewards—make them instant, and don't be stingy. Your brain needs them. And I promise (well, Volkow, Schlund, Wexler, and Fleshner promise) it gets easier. That's not a bunch of self-help nonsense. It's biology."
>
> *Here's the link to the full article:*
> *http://www.oprah.com/article/omagazine/omag_200701_change/1*

What is the dopamine system referred to by Ms Skloot? Human brains are wired to promote activities that help us survive, such as procreation and eating. When we engage in these activities, our brains release a wonderful substance called dopamine. Think of dopamine as your internal chocolate - or whatever you eat to feel really good. That is why food – which produces dopamine - is such a powerful reward and nearly impossible to ignore! To rewire a habit, you must rewire your reward and give yourself another stimulus that is better for you.

For instance, imagine you are sitting in front of your computer cruising the internet. Clicking away is fun and your brain releases a little bit of dopamine.

Your list of Marketing Me activities says *"Call someone in my network to discuss my contributions to the ACT! project."*

You glance at this list and WHOOPS the dopamine disappears! Something else usually kicks in: Adrenaline. You *really* do not want to make those calls. You are afraid you will meet resistance and fear makes your body release adrenaline. (Remember fight or flight?)

> *He who is afraid of a thing gives it power over him.*
> *Moorish Proverb*

To overcome that adrenaline and get rid of your fear, you must boost your dopamine level. So, give yourself a powerful reward for making that call.

What reward works? First, it has to be specific to you, and, to keep you healthy, should not be food. It also has to be easy and immediate, especially when you are first making change (within that initial 30 day window.)

Some good examples of dopamine producing rewards:
- A deep breath and full body stretch that lasts at least 30 seconds
- Chatting with a friendly colleague
- Chew a piece of tasty gum or piece of sugarless candy
- Buy yourself a newspaper and read the sports (or funnies!)
- Go outside and shoot some baskets (or toss a few into your waste basket)
- Play a video game (briefly)
- Take a walk around the block – or other quick exercise
- Read a joke – laugh out loud
- Reread an encouraging note or card
- Look at funny pictures on the web (my favorite is www.Icanhascheezburger.com)
- Hug someone
- Hit the driving range or putt in your cubby

Do as many of these as often as you need in order to keep the dopamine pump going while you are establishing your new habit. Eventually, your brain will be rewired to anticipate pleasure from completing that new habit and you will feel the "buzz" just thinking about doing it. It takes time and determined effort and the effort is worth it because this method does work.

> *Never let the fear of striking out get in your way.*
> George Herman "Babe" Ruth

A winning environment

In their recent book, <u>Influencer,</u> Patterson, et al, outlined six different strategies that, when implemented in concert, create permanent, powerful change. They say you can zero in on and change a key behavior by involving not only your mindset, but by making a few crucial changes in both your social and physical environment. Read the book to get the full story. The key element is that change is possible. Change takes a concerted effort and one of the things you *have* to change is your environment. Just like the dieters who need to avoid temptations, surround yourself with successful people you want to emulate, imitate what they do, put into practice the tools that work, and get rid of any distractions that might derail your progress.

For instance, to make certain you are consistently promoting yourself in many different arenas, you must calendar and track your activities. (Reread <u>Chapter 5</u> to remind yourself of the benefits and necessity of tracking your Marketing Me campaign.) Put in place a user-friendly tracking system and keep it handy. Schedule time everyday to update your calendar. That is a change to your environment. How many other systems can you put in place to support your campaign? The more, the better.

Zero is a number.

Tom had not been able to figure out how to get organized since his job responsibilities increased after a lay-off. His desk was covered in piles of project folders, his email box was never empty, and he had unreturned phone call dating back 3 months. Taking our advice, Tom started one new habit: For every organizing activity he did he rewarded himself with a cup of fresh coffee or water and a walk around the block. He responded to emails at 6 AM, returned phone calls one hour each day, used 30 minutes to prioritize unscheduled projects and then scheduled time to work on them. Within 20 days, Tom's desk was clear and his email inbox was empty by the end of the day. He had some lapses when he skipped a day or two, but the steadiness of choosing an activity, scheduling time to do it and scheduling time to reward himself, created a new rhythm and stronger sense of control for Tom. His boss, stopping by his office, remarked, "Tom, I'm really impressed with how you've changed your work habits recently. I know you have a lot on your plate. If you can teach me some of that, I'd be indebted. How about we set up a time for you to show me what you're doing?"

Create your environment promoting the activities that get results. Clear you desk and your desktop of junk that distracts you, keeping only those things that inspire and motivate you. Add reminders that help you get the results you want.

The new picture of yourself

Another key in devoting yourself to behavioral change is through constant reminders of the new *you*. You need to attack change with regular physical actions, auditory reinforcement and visual cues. I have already addressed the physical actions: Act as if.

Think about these questions:

> Mirror, mirror on the wall...

- How do you see yourself in your successful future? What desk are you at? What do you see when you look up? What are you wearing?
- Are you favored by your boss, getting great assignments and challenging opportunities to grow?
- Do you see yourself sitting at the table in meetings with decision makers, actively participating in discussions and influencing decisions?
- How much has your income increased?
- What does your boss tell you about your next advancement and promotion?
- Do your colleagues seek your advice and knowledge?
- Are you included in email correspondences about important projects?
- Is your calendar full of appointments with important people and vital project meetings?
- Have you been invited to company strategy meetings?
- Do you get requests to contribute articles to the company newsletter?
- How many articles have you published in your professional journal?
- Do quotes from you get into press releases about your projects or company?

Record yourself answering these questions. Create a story of the new, more retainable you. Listen to this recording often: everyday for 30 days is, of course, my recommendation.

Purposeful visualization is one of our brain's most powerful and underutilized tools. Harness this by practicing visualization daily. There is literally no limit to what your mind can help you achieve.

Tell others how you see yourself: declare this vision out loud repeatedly. Visualize the kind of work you want to be doing as if you are already doing it.

Clearly imagine the people you talk to everyday, the projects you work on, the great results you produce. Rehearse this vision everyday. A great time to do it is 1-2 minutes lying in bed after the alarm goes off and before you actually spring up for the day. Play the movie of your upgraded life on the inside of your eyelids.

Use the energy and inspiration it gives you to persevere at your Marketing Me activities which help you make your vision a reality.

Summary

In this chapter I revealed ways that you might create your own hurdles for initiating and maintaining your Marketing Me campaign. I offered tools, tactics and encouragement to get going, keep going and keep your job.

The rest is up to you!

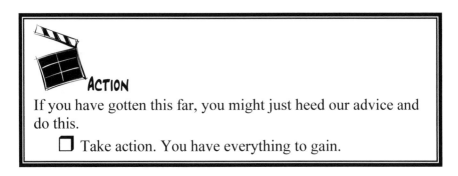

ACTION

If you have gotten this far, you might just heed our advice and do this.

☐ Take action. You have everything to gain.

Epilogue: What If You Lose Your Job Anyway?

Despite your efforts, your job has been eliminated and you are out looking for the next opportunity. There are many resources out there for launching a job search, building a resume, and boning up on interview skills.

Resources developed in your Marketing Me campaign

First, it is worthwhile to inventory what you did to keep your job, assuming you followed my recommendations in this book. Many of those activities are useful for your job-seeking project.

For instance:
- You have collected testimonials from colleagues and coworkers as to the value of your contributions.
    - You can use these as reference letters
- You have logged your project work and results
    - Excellent data for your new resume
- You built your own performance review
    - Vital information for cover letters and answering interview questions
- You created a personal marketing message
    - Perfect for including in your personal email signature and putting on your job-seeking business cards
- You have established self-promotion habits
    - A solid foundation upon which to build productive job-seeking habits

Moving on

After getting laid off, you can expect to go through an adjustment in your thinking and your schedule. Even if your company offers an outplacement service, the road to your new job is in your hands, as we asserted about your job preservation campaign. Use the scheduling and discipline skills that you learned while implementing Marketing Me and get to work. Your interim job is to find a new job.

While some people take getting laid off in stride and quickly get into a new life rhythm, others struggle with resentment, anger, thoughts of vengeance, and situational depression. We encourage you to acknowledge that job-seeking is a tough transition and if you need help seek it. Do not wallow or fester. It will only interfere with your efforts to get a different job.

Complaints about the company that laid you off are not the kinds of statements you want creeping into interviews. So if you find yourself unable to bite your tongue then talk to a professional. Your former employer may refer you to resources, such as an Employee Assistance Program (EAP) during the first 90 days after your lay off. Use it if you need it. If your company does not, then seek out a career counselor or therapist. Ask friends, family and former colleagues for referrals. Do not rely on the Yellow Pages or internet ads.

> Fortes Fortuna Adiuvat
> *Latin for:*
> Fortune Favors the Brave

Job search resources

Once you know you have to find a job, start looking at the job search websites. Here are a few:
- www.theladders.com/ (for jobs over $100,000)
- www.jobsdirectusa.com/ (Started by a former AIG employee)
- www.monster.com/
- www.simplyhired.com
- www.job.com (For local job searches)
- http://hotjobs.yahoo.com/
- http://www.job-search-engine.com/
- www.Dice.com (for technology jobs)
- www.careerbuilder.com

- www.business.com (For construction jobs)
- www.upmo.com (to assess your network)

Go to this URL to learn how each site ranks:
- http://www.consumersearch.com/job-sites

Use your Network

Keep in mind that these job search sites usually allow only blind applications meaning you never get the name of a real person to whom you are submitting your resume. So, you can not address your cover letter to an individual or follow-up with a specific person. While some people are fortunate enough to get hired from a blind submission, it is unlikely.

Tip: *While job search sites can tell you what kinds of jobs are being filled at any point in time, the best job seeking resource is your network of colleagues outside your company. Find a reason to keep in touch with them at least twice a month during a job search.*

Your network of professional colleagues, friends and family will *always* be a better source for job openings and referrals. Talk to people everyday and follow up with consistent vigor. Tell them about job postings you see online and ask who they know at those companies. Persistence pays off more than vast quantity of resumes submitted.

Resumes and Interviewing

Go here to see how some resume writing services rank:

- http://www.best10resumewriters.com

And, finally, here are some resources for improving interviewing skills:

- http://www.job-interview.net/
- www.secretstogettinghired.com (Free booklet and offers for paid job search resources)

Most of the job search sites have additional links or pages that lead to advice about resumes, cover letters, on-line job application tips, interviewing tools and more. Most of it is free and worth exploring.

More Marketing Me resources

Consider me, Doug, part of your Marketing Me tool kit and give me a call. I am well-versed in surfing the corporate environment, understanding and working with entrepreneurial personalities, recovering from a lay-off, and searching for the next job. I can refer you to coaching and consulting services to help you implement the concepts in Marketing Me and get results. I can also help you find specific professional development coaching that goes beyond what is in this book.

Contact information is on these websites:

- www.MarketingMe.US
- www.MarketingMeBook.com